Michael New
Mercenary...
or American Soldier?

New, Daniel D.
    Michael New : Mercenary-- or American soldier? /
[Daniel New ; with Cliff Kincaid]. -- 2nd ed.
    p. cm.
    Includes bibliographical references.
    ISBN: 0-966813-2-0

    1. New, Michael G.-- Trials, litigation, etc.
2. Trials (Military offenses)--United States.
3. United Nations--Armed Forces.   I. Kincaid,
Cliff. II. Title.

Daniel D. New

The father of Army Specialist Michael G. New, Daniel is a Christian without apology, and a fourth generation Texan without apology. Until recent years, he was an American without apology, but our so-called "leaders" have become a world-wide embarrassment to any decent American traveling abroad.

Daniel writes and lectures extensively on a wide variety of topics. He and his wife, Suzanne, have homeschooled their seven children (a medium-sized family) while living in Texas, Papua New Guinea, New Zealand and The Philippines. He is an ornamental horticulturist by training, an amateur linguist, an avid gardener and poultryman by avocation, a patent-holding inventor, and an avid student of the "Literature of Freedom."

The **Michael New Action Fund** is responsible for the legal defense for Michael New, as well as a world-wide public education effort to teach concerned citizens about what is happening to national sovereignty. They have one documentary video available, *GOOD CONDUCT, The Story of Michael New*.

To contact Daniel or Michael New:

> **Michael New Action Fund**
> P.O. Box 100
> Iredell, Texas 76649

Visit MNAF on-line at: http://www.mikenew.com/
E-mail Daniel at: ddnew@bigfoot.com

Cliff Kincaid

President, America's Survival
Director, American Sovereignty Action Project

Cliff is the chief organizer of the Coalition for the American Sovereignty and Bill of Rights, which includes more than 50 organizations opposing the International Criminal Court. He lectures widely and serves as a consultant on international affairs.

Books by Cliff Kincaid include:
Global Bondage: The U.N. Plan to Rule the World
Global Taxes for World Government

Videos include:
Justice for the World, or Global Terror
(on the International Criminal Court)
Who Runs the Global Economy?
(on global taxes and global economic instability)

To order Cliff's books, tapes or other
materials, call 410-535-7168; or write to:
    Cliff Kincaid
    P.O. Box 146
    Owings, Maryland 20736

Visit Cliff's web site at: http://www.usasurvival.org
E-mail Cliff Kincaid at antiun@earthlink.net

CONTENTS

Michael and Claudia New
May 1998

INTRODUCTION

On October 10, 1995, the 1/15 Battalion of the 3rd Infantry Division of the U.S. Army came to attention at 0900 in Schweinfurt, Germany. All but one of the 550 soldiers were wearing a sky-blue baseball-style cap with a United Nations insignia on the front. One was wearing the olive-drab flat cap that is authorized to be worn with the Battle Dress Uniform. With this simple act of disobeying a direct order, Spc. 4 Michael New set the stage for a legal battle that has profound implications for the future of American generations. At issue is the authority of the President of the United States to order American soldiers into service under the United Nations without the constitutional permission of Congress.

America stands at a crossroads in history. Will we face the future as an independent Republic? Or will our grandchildren grow up in a New World Order governed from New York City, where we as a Member State, can be consistently outvoted by a hundred other countries who do not share our heritage, our values, and our interest? This legal case may well determine the future of our nation.

Chapter 1

"I THINK I'M GOING TO BE COURT-MARTIALED"

August 21, 1995

The call was unexpected. Michael, calling from Germany, where he was stationed, had phoned us over the weekend, and we didn't think he would be calling again on a Monday morning.

"Dad," he said, "I think I'm going to be court-martialed."

These words stuck into me like a knife. "What on earth have you done?" I asked.

"I haven't done anything," he said. "It's for something I'm not going to do. They've told me that I have to wear the United Nations uniform on our coming deployment into Macedonia, and I told them I have a problem with that order." Later, he added, "You know, Dad, if they can force me to wear that blue helmet in Europe, then what's to keep them from forcing me to wear it someday in Texas or some other state? The real question is one of authority — where do they get it?"

These statements put Michael right in the middle of a debate which continues over the meaning of his oath, which consists of the following:

> "I do solemnly swear that I will support and defend the Constitution of the United States against all enemies, foreign and domestic; that I will bear true faith and allegiance to the same; and that I will obey the orders of the President of the United States and the orders of the officers appointed over me, according to regulations and the uniform code of military justice.

So help me God."[1]

I'm often asked if we are bitter or angry over our son Michael being prosecuted for refusing to wear a United Nations uniform and refusing to report to a foreign military commander. Some people think we ought to be completely disgusted with a system that punished my son, a soldier with an excellent service record and a promising military career, for standing up for America, his oath, and against United Nations control of our troops. I wouldn't be honest if I didn't say that I've shaken my head in disbelief, even dismay, over how our nation has come to this point. But we hope and pray that the case of Army Specialist Michael New can help to turn our country around. It will take years, but I'm convinced that if the American people appreciate and understand this case, there will be a growing tide of opposition against the pretenders in power who are subverting our constitutional republic.

My own father, Clyde New[2], used to emphasize that standing up for freedom is the responsibility of all citizens, and is not an action or an event – that it is instead a lifestyle – a commitment upon which our national freedom depends. If enough citizens just go along to get along, "go with the flow," and take the easy road, then this Republic will die.

These are not empty words. They are a recognition of what this case represents. All of our most cherished values — freedom, family, service, sacrifice, sovereignty and independence - are wrapped up in this case. I recognize there are those who believe that it simply involves a case of a soldier who was punished for disobeying an order. But I challenge those holding this belief to take another look – to understand who Michael is, and who we are — his family, friends, allies and supporters. We are the American people. And we want our country back.

There are those who expect that the treatment of Michael

---

[1] "Your Oath. Defending the Constitution. Our Common Bond." Deputy Chief of Staff for Personnel, The Pentagon, Washington, D.C. 20310.

[2] Clyde Wayne New, USMC 1942-1945. American patriot. Eighty years old as this book is written.

has shaken our faith in America and its institutions. But, because our faith is in a Supreme Creator, and because we understand the sinful nature of a fallen mankind, we are not surprised when men assume power and then quickly find themselves wallowing in the corruption which Lord Acton so accurately predicted.

The arrogance of this administration in turning over our sovereignty is not the only controversy that has drawn attention to the fact that corruption has infected our governmental institutions. It would take more than a chapter just to list them, and there are books upon books available on that subject. The Clinton-Gore Administration has raised arrogant lawlessness to an unprecedented level.

What has happened to Michael New is part of a pattern. An administration which orders a young soldier to report to the U.N. will sell our sovereignty to the United Nations and our security to China. Indeed, if the U.S. Congress had come to the defense of Michael New in a more forthright manner, we might have been spared some of these other foreign policy scandals, in which foreign interests have been placed above American interests.

But the treatment of Michael New has made White House corruption into a very personal matter for us. The controversy has caused me, my wife Suzanne, and our entire family extreme anguish. But the anguish is not simply for Michael New. It's for our dying Republic. Yes, it's painful to look into Michael's eyes, knowing that his promising military career was cut short, and that his bad conduct discharge has left him, as Geoffrey Botkin so eloquently stated, "…with a stigma that will follow him all the rest of his life."[3]

Suzanne and I have mingled our prayers and our tears for Michael. But we also cry for our country – and for future generations. We are encouraged by the example that he has set in sacrificing his military career in the hopes that America's sons

[3] The documentary video, *GOOD CONDUCT, The Story of Michael New*, is available through the Michael New Action Fund, P.O. Box 100, Iredell, Texas 76649.

can once again serve an American-led and American-controlled military.

When Suzanne was being interviewed for the videotape, *Good Conduct*, about Michael's case, she said, "This has been a hard time for our family to go through because parents don't like to see their children suffer. We suffer when they suffer. However, we're really proud of Michael for standing up for principles that we taught him. We're proud of him for having firm moral convictions based on truth – what is right. We're proud of him for being willing to stand up against a lot of opposition. It's not easy when your case is named the United States Government vs. Specialist New. That's rather daunting. I really hope and pray that Michael's stand will in some way awaken the American people to recognize that our nation seems to be in peril."

I remain optimistic, and I am not afraid to say so publicly. At a national conference sponsored by the *American Sovereignty Action Project,* organized by my friend and book collaborator Cliff Kincaid, I said, "Don't feel sorry for Michael New. He gets to stand up with Patrick Henry, Nathan Hale, and George Washington and say, 'I love my country.'"

By taking his stand against the U.N., Michael certainly didn't give his life or shed his blood on a battlefield. But his decision, taken after careful consideration, consultations, and with divine guidance, was nevertheless momentous. Trying to put aside my self-interest, I truly believe that years from now, the case of Michael New will be viewed in historical terms as a constitutional crisis — one that bears on the fate and future of our nation in the same way that our founders took their stand against King George.

The truth is, I have never been more inspired by any person in American history than my own son. To some, this may sound like over-heated rhetoric from a proud father. And certainly a father's pride enters into such a statement. Michael is a human being, and we recognize that he is not perfect. But his case, which is on-going and by no means settled, has the potential to alter the course of history, to serve as a rallying cry for Americans today as we are faced with coming to grips with "old-fashioned" concepts such as national independence, freedom and sovereignty. It's far bigger than the individuals involved.

The outcome of the case, though disappointing in so many respects, has also been a positive experience. It proved that Michael, who was taught love for country and love for God, had become "a bright light in a dark place." From the personal point of view of a father, can there be any greater reward than for a son or daughter to do what is right? In this day and age, when so many young people have lost hope, direction and vision, Michael exhibited courage, faith and patriotism. Isn't this what we as parents and grandparents want from our children and grandchildren?

Yet Michael's courage was not welcomed in the ranks of the military, the government or even the media. He had focused the spotlight on a policy that was being carried out largely behind-the-scenes. Media coverage of the case is particularly interesting.

My Lai and Hugh Thompson

Dale Robertson, Administrative Trustee for the Michael New Action Fund, points out that, "…[W]hile many elements of the liberal media treated Michael with disdain or contempt, they have celebrated Hugh Thompson as a hero." Thompson is the former U.S. Army helicopter pilot who, on March 6, 1998, received the prestigious Soldier's Medal for his efforts to halt the bloodshed at the My Lai massacre in Vietnam nearly 30 years ago. He's been called "The Forgotten Hero of My Lai" in a book about the case. What he did was rescue at least 10 Vietnamese civilians and threaten to use deadly force against Americans troops who were apparently willing to obey an illegal order — an order to kill those civilians.

In presenting the award to Thompson and door gunner Lawrence Colburn at the Vietnam Veterans Memorial, Army Major General Michael Ackerman described the My Lai massacre as "one of the most shameful chapters in the Army's history."[4]

The treatment of Specialist Michael New is another shameful chapter.

It is important, however, to recall what happened at My Lai, a village in Vietnam, and what this means for the U.S. Armed Forces today. My Lai was the scene of a horrible massacre — killings that sickened all Americans. Platoon leader Army Lt. William Calley was convicted and sentenced to jail for his role in the massacre. But despite what the media have said about My Lai, what happened there did not involve typical soldiers who had been trained to kill innocent people. My Lai didn't represent U.S. policy. It was an aberration. A formal Army inquiry determined that the troops went out of control largely because of poor training. Company C of the 11th Infantry Brigade had been sent to Vietnam a month early, which meant cutting the final training period from eight to four weeks. The unit lacked order, discipline and cohesion.

My Lai stands as a reminder of what can go wrong in war, even when our own beloved American soldiers are involved. It also stands as a reminder that our soldiers are not under any obligation to obey illegal orders. Indeed, the lesson is that they should not obey such orders, that they have a sacred and moral responsibility to reject such orders. The massacre at My Lai took place in the context of American soldiers who were obviously angry at the deaths and maimings of their comrades. The enemy in Vietnam was a vicious and sometimes invisible foe. But what those troops did was morally wrong, and they had to be held accountable.

Michael New did not intervene to stop a massacre, and we

4 www.archive.abcnews.com/sections/us%5Cdailynews/vietnam

don't argue that he deserved any particular award for what he did. But he certainly should not have been court-martialed. In retrospect, the Army, though under White House pressure, should have recognized that his cause was both legally and morally right. The facts demonstrate that he disobeyed an order, but it was an illegal order. This is apparent to anyone who seriously and objectively examines the facts of this case. The blunt truth is that he was ordered to participate in an illegal and unconstitutional foreign military operation.

But as Hugh Thompson was honored 30 years after the fact for his stand at My Lai, perhaps it may take 30 or more years to recognize what Michael has accomplished.

Readers of this book should understand that Thompson received his Soldier's Medal only after a concerted campaign was waged on his behalf. Congressional letters helped put pressure on the Army to review the case. We have to see comparable pressure exerted on the Armed Forces in Michael's case, although ultimately the resolution may take place in the Congressional arena. Michael's military career is over, but we want justice for Michael because of what it will represent for those who remain in the Armed Forces, and for those who come after him. Final justice in the Michael New case will mean that the character and integrity of the Armed Forces will have been restored.

One element of the short-term tragedy is that because of what happened to Michael, we can no longer recommend military service for any of our sons. I have encouraged them to refuse or postpone enlistment in the Armed Services until such time as we can find out who they are going to be serving. I give this advice, publicly, to young people who ask me about enlisting, and then I ask them to be sure and tell their Congressmen what they have done.

The sacred oath of a soldier doesn't mean anything if it can be taken and put on a shelf and then you can be forced to do something else. Under the Clinton-Gore Administration and a compliant Congress, this situation still exists. A U.S. soldier can still be ordered at any time to drop his allegiance to the U.S. Constitution and function as a mercenary for the U.N.

It is with a heavy heart that I offer this advice to young people today. Obviously, we need soldiers to defend America. But if they are not going to defend their own country, their own borders or their own national interests, then why should we encourage our young people to join? This is the dilemma we currently face as a people and a country. Our national security and sovereignty are on the line. How have we come to this point in our history?

A Pentagon booklet about the oath says, "Twenty-three of the fifty signers of the Constitution were veterans of the Revolutionary War. After distinguishing themselves in combat, they went on to serve in the newly established government, as patriots and leaders. When taking the oath, you accept the same demands now that American soldiers and army civilians have embodied since the Revolutionary War. The oath deals with values and ethics....These citizen soldiers embodied another set of values including loyalty, duty, selfless service, and integrity. These attributes are collectively referred to as the Army ethic. By instilling these four individual values within each soldier and Army civilian, we can strengthen the professional Army ethic."

To Michael, an order to wear a U.N. uniform, the uniform of what is undeniably a foreign power, is a strike at the very heart of freedom. He was faced with a critical decision. One thing he knew was that his oath was sacred.

The U.S. Constitution carried this patriotic impulse one step further, declaring in Article 1, Section 9 that no U.S. official or officer "shall, without the consent of Congress, accept any present, Emolument, Office, or Title, of any kind whatsoever, from any King, prince or foreign state." This was a categorical statement designed to prevent our Armed Forces and other U.S. officials from coming under the influence or control of a foreign state or entity. The acceptance of foreign badges or foreign titles was viewed as a sign that the individual wearing them was switching allegiance and losing fidelity to the United States. The Constitution was clear that an exception could be made only with the consent of Congress.

One may notice that the sacred nature of the oath — the phrase "So help me God" — has remained consistent. In "An Officer's Oath," an article in the Military Law Review of July 1964, Lt. Col. Thomas Reese explained that the oath "is a pledge to perform an act faithfully and truthfully...The attestation involves the principle of invoking God to witness that which is announced as the truth, and implied is the invocation of His vengeance, or renunciation of favor, in the event of falsehood." Reese noted the religious significance of the oath by quoting a Biblical passage which declared that "if a man...swear an oath to bind his soul with a bond; he shall not break his word, he shall do according to all that proceedeth out of his mouth." (Numbers 30:2)

Hence, all soldiers, including Michael, take a sacred oath which invites divine judgment if they fail to carry out their duty and obligation. This made the oath very special to him. While they may just be words to many who take such an oath, they had meaning to Michael. It has been a characteristic of our family that we prefer to serve our Creator and our Savior first and foremost, and let the approval of men be secondary.

There is no dispute that Michael was given an order to wear the U.N. uniform. And it is also true that he disobeyed this order. The key question in Michael's case was whether the order was legal or illegal.

The same question applies to U.N. deployments of U.S. troops today. The overwhelming evidence which has been assembled in Michael's case demonstrates that such an order was and is illegal. What is astonishing is not that Michael took his stand but that more soldiers have not followed his lead.

One explanation, of course, lies in the fact that the "bait-and-switch" — of U.S. soldiers being deployed as U.N. troops — happens in a way that is not supposed to provoke controversy. Another factor is the need for more and better education of our young people, especially on the law and the Constitution. This is something that will certainly change as more people, including those in our Armed Services, become aware of the true facts in the Michael New case. Our hope is that this book will find its way into the hands of many of the very patriotic Americans still serving in our Armed Forces.

The oath expresses a level of support for the Constitution that is not conditional. In other words, it does not say that a soldier supports the Constitution depending on whether certain conditions are met. However, the reference to following orders is conditional. It doesn't say that a soldier obeys all orders, period. It says a soldier obeys orders "according to regulations and the Uniform Code of Military Justice." In other words, the orders have to be lawful and consistent with the Constitution.

The question is frequently asked: how did Michael know it was an illegal order? Further, as one military judge put it, "Why did he think it was patently illegal?" Sometimes, the question is asked in a manner that is intended to suggest that Michael had no reason on earth to doubt the legality of this order. In other words, how could a young soldier have had the state of mind to question such a command? Who did he think he was? I think the question is sometimes asked out of embarrassment because others, including high-ranking military officers, didn't ask it before, and they should have. Indeed, it's a sad commentary on the state of our uniformed services that it was left to a 22 year-old Army specialist, to ask such a basic and profound question.

A Question of Obedience

Clearly, a soldier cannot pick and choose the orders he wants to obey. Good order and discipline are absolutely necessary to a professional military unit. If lives are on the line, orders that seem designed to save lives are presumed to be lawful. On the other hand, a soldier should not have to be told that he can question an order only if he has years of legal training and the mind of a Supreme Court justice. In Michael's case, his doubt about the order was prompted by a combination of factors, including instinct, training, education, background and knowledge of the military.

Another factor was his Christian orientation. Michael had a basic understanding that the order was wrong. Was God talking to him? Was his decision-making process guided by God? Had God somehow selected Michael to make a stand not only for America but for the Lord Himself? These questions might strike some as wild and irrelevant. But we believe that God works in mysterious ways in the lives of individuals and nations. In this case, I do not think it is an understatement to say that Michael was and is performing a sacred mission. Today, of course, the issue has grown far beyond the particular circumstances of one soldier. Since Michael's case garnered national and even international attention, the matter of the U.N.'s growing authority and power in foreign affairs has taken on more urgency and significance.

U.N. Secretary-General Kofi Annan even refers to the U.N. being the "ultimate power" in the world, with U.S. troops functioning as U.N. "peacekeepers."

On a critical level, of course, any soldier or veteran knows that the military uniform is extremely important in several different ways. First, it represents the Armed Services of the United States and one's branch of service. Second, it contains the awards and medals and other identification that are unique to that American soldier. Scandals have occurred over the unauthorized use of such awards and medals, undermining and even ruining military careers. Even without consulting law books, Army regulations or the constitution itself, Michael understood that an order to alter that uniform was of monumental significance. Every soldier knows this.

"A lot of good men have bled in the same uniform for my country and I'm not willing to take it off now to fight for some foreign government that doesn't have my ideals at heart," Michael was recalling the order to wear the U.N. uniform. "I think that's disrespectful to all the veterans, all the people who died fighting for America."

In Michael's case, he was ordered to make significant alterations in his Army Battle Dress Uniform. He was ordered to remove his United States Flag patch from the dominant right shoulder and place it on the left shoulder. The U.S. flag was to be replaced by a United Nations patch. This was a message to our soldiers that the U.S. Army had become, in effect, a unit of the U.N. Army. He was also ordered to wear various other U.N. accessories, including a blue cap, beret or helmet, and a blue scarf.

Michael knew that the Army's Battle Dress Uniform (BDU) he had been wearing was authorized. But he had no evidence to believe or suspect that the changes he was ordered to make in that uniform were authorized. Furthermore, he understood that removing a U.S. flag and replacing it with a symbol of another organization would undermine the sacred oath he had already taken in joining the Army in the first place. Common sense told him that the Army had not abandoned the Stars and Stripes. These considerations were reason enough to question the order.

Not only was Michael being ordered to wear a U.N. uniform, he was being ordered to deploy to Macedonia, part of the former Yugoslavia, where he would be under the control of General Jehu Engstrom of Finland. General Engstrom had said about his position, "This is a very unique and historic opportunity. Before Macedonia, a non-American or non-NATO officer has never before had command of an American battalion abroad." Clearly, General Engstrom recognized the significance of the moment. He was taking command of Americans, putting them at his disposal. The U.S. Army claimed he was only assuming "operational control" of U.S. troops, a vague formulation that confuses the issue. This is mere semantic wrangling.

For his part, Michael was supposed to wear the uniform of a foreign organization and take orders from a foreigner. How on earth could such an order be legal or constitutional when directed at a soldier who had taken a sacred oath to defend the U.S. Constitution? On its face, the order was illegal, even patently illegal.

As Michael said, "I was taught and believe that the Constitution is the fundamental law of America, and if there is any ambiguity or conflict with the U.N. or any treaty or international agreement or organization, then the U.S. Constitution would always prevail. My Army enlistment oath is to the Constitution. I cannot find any reference to the United Nations in that oath."

When he enlisted into the Army in February of 1993, the Army recruiter in Conroe, Texas, had never mentioned U.N. command, foreign officers or wearing a U.N. uniform. Instead, he was told that he was signing up for the U.S. military.

I have said that if the U.N. wants to recruit our soldiers, it should do so openly by setting up recruitment centers in our cities and towns. Then we could see, openly and above-board, whether our young people want to serve their own country, or as U.N. mercenaries. But I was being facetious in this remark. I doubt that it would be legal, and Americans who volunteer to serve in the foreign military of any power, says the

Constitution, risk losing their American citizenship. In any case, Americans should not be tricked into serving the U.N. after they have voluntarily signed up for the U.S. Armed Forces.

The year 1998 is the 25th anniversary of the all-volunteer Army. A visit to the Army web site (www.goarmy.com) in June of 1998 discloses that recruits are still not being told that they may be called upon to serve the U.N. In the section on recruitment, young men and women are told that they will "make a contribution to the nation's defense," but there is nothing about the U.N. There are, however, references to signing up for the Army and getting an education, adventure, and money. A photo on the web site, which was also featured in Army newspaper advertisements, depicted eight Army soldiers — none of them in U.N. uniforms.

Even though the order to serve the U.N. struck Michael as flatly wrong, he immediately went to his superior officers asking for the authority or justification for the order. He was told to study the U.N. Charter, to disabuse him of the notion that the world body represented a foreign power, organization or government. But this backfired and only reinforced Michael's position and concern. Michael studied the document and concluded that the U.N. was, indeed, very much like a world government, with a legislative body, courts, and sources of funding.

Before the court martial, Michael said, "Two additional elements the U.N. needs to become the One World Government are (1) world taxes, which are already in the works, and (2) a world army." He continued, "And that's what they're trying to make me."

At one point, Michael was told the order to wear a U.N. uniform was lawful because, "The President says so, therefore it is." But nobody provided a legitimate, legal or rationale basis for the order. Eventually, a battalion briefing about the deployment offered the justification that, "We wear the U.N. uniform because it looks fabulous." Michael smiled without humor as he recalled that briefing, "I didn't think that was very funny."

...because they look fabulous!

Indeed, it was an attempt to mock and intimidate an honest citizen-soldier who had asked a legitimate question, to coerce him into dropping his objections and falling in line. It is truly a tragedy that the issue of maintaining one's allegiance to the U.S. Constitution should earn one such scorn from officers who themselves took a similar oath of allegiance.

"In about two months' time," Michael recalled, "no one gave me an answer, and so on October 10, the day we were supposed to be in formation in our U.N. uniforms, I showed up in my regulation U.S. Army uniform." However, some 549 U.S. Army soldiers did show up in formation, wearing a United Nations emblem on their baby-blue caps and U.N. patches on their right shoulders! Michael was immediately removed from the parade ground, where he was informed that he would be facing a court-martial. He was read his rights. And this began the chain of events that continues sending shock waves around the country and the world.

After Michael was removed from the formation, the remaining U.S. soldiers came to attention and saluted General Jehu Engstrom, of Finland, their new commanding officer for the next six months. General Engstrom, like other U.N. officers, had taken a pledge of allegiance to the U.N.

This critical piece of information bears repeating: the Army failed over a period of six weeks to rationally explain why the order was legal. Instead, it resorted to absurd claims and harassment.

Besides the absurd rationale that the U.N. uniforms "look fabulous," Michael was subjected to a whispering campaign. One sergeant reportedly referred to him as a "spineless wimp," suggesting that his real objection to carrying out the order was fear of possibly seeing military action. Michael's compatriots knew this was completely false. Until he heard of the uniform switch, Michael had been looking forward to the deployment. At the time, Macedonia was considered to be close to military action in the former Yugoslavia, where the civil war in Bosnia had taken thousands of lives, and some military hostilities had been reported in the area. But it was not directly in a war zone.

It was, of course, never Michael's intention to avoid a military conflict. Indeed, he had been decorated for his service in a Persian Gulf deployment called Operation Southern Watch to Kuwait in 1993. Although this occurred after the end of the Persian Gulf war, it was still a volatile area. This deployment also demonstrated another critical fact — that Michael's key objection was not to serving in a U.N.-authorized operation but in a U.N.-controlled operation. Operation Southern Watch was authorized or endorsed by the U.N. but Michael served in an American uniform under an unbroken chain of American command.

It is also important to remember that Michael's decision not to wear the U.N. uniform was not life-threatening to himself or anybody else. There was no possible way that it could be argued that his action was risky or hazardous. He didn't announce this decision during the heat of battle when lives were on the line.

What's more, Michael offered to accept a transfer to another unit or an honorable discharge. Nevertheless, the Army decided to make an example out of him. I believe that this decision had to be approved at the highest levels of the U.S. Government, probably in the White House itself. If President Clinton did not personally approve Michael's prosecution, then the decision was taken by other White House and civilian and military officials who clearly understood that this was the "politically correct" thing to do. They had to realize that this one young man was standing in the way of the "New World Order" that so many people have been talking and warning about. This explains why they could not permit him to transfer to another unit or take an honorable discharge. If any soldier could refuse induction into the U.N. Army, the floodgates would be opened and others — hundreds if not thousands — could follow his lead. So they determined to make an example of Michael New.

Michael's court-martial proceeded on the basis that he had violated Article 92 of the Uniform Code of Military Justice (UCMJ) by disobeying a lawful order. During the court-martial, the Army finally offered a rationale for claiming the order was legal. It cited Article 11, Section 2 of the Constitution, establishing the president as Commander-in-Chief; the U.N. Participation Act; and the Foreign Assistance Act. However, there is nothing in any of these constitutional provisions or statutes which justify ordering our troops to wear U.N. uniforms and serve U.N. commanders. Indeed, as Michael's lawyers have convincingly argued, the Constitution, the U.N. Participation Act, and the Foreign Assistance Act either prohibit such deployments or do not authorize them. What's more, there is no authorization for all or any part of the U.N. uniform in Army regulations. These are absolutely critical facts.

In any event, the critical thing to keep in mind is that when Michael went on trial, all of the evidence assembled by his lawyers, demonstrating that he was justified in disobeying an unlawful and unconstitutional order, was excluded. The judge didn't want this evidence presented to the jury. Furthermore, the military judge determined for himself and the jury that the order was lawful. Having been told that they could not look at the evidence, the jury did the only thing they could under the circumstances — they found him guilty of disobeying an order. B١ ׃ rather than give him a dishonorable discharge, they gave him a bad conduct discharge (BCD). This may have reflected their uneasiness over the trial itself, and their nagging suspicion that they weren't being told the whole truth about the matter. Incredibly, in the military appeals court, the U.S. Government has not contested the unlawfulness of the order. Instead, it has argued that the question of its legality is a political issue and that it only needs to prove that Michael violated an order.

What is happening here? The bottom line is that the courts, both civilian and military, do not want to address the most critical issue — that President Clinton has violated the law and the Constitution. In short, they don't want to come to grips with the fact that we are in the midst of a constitutional crisis. By labeling it "political," they hope they don't have to deal with it — at least for now. In a crucial sense, of course, it is political. Congress has the constitutional responsibility to hold President Clinton accountable through impeachment proceedings. The question that we will continue to ask is, why hasn't he been held accountable?

Michael's case, which is still alive in the courts, has to be fought through to its ultimate conclusion, even if it does have political implications.

In our case, we knew we had to fight it, and that we had to assemble the best legal minds that were available. The first step was to find legal representation. I began to phone friends, who recommended lawyers. They all said, "Money." We had no money. Within a week or so, I received a call from Major Chuck Johnson (USMC. Res.), who recommended Ronald D. Ray, a retired Marine colonel, practicing law in Kentucky. Colonel Ray had served under President Reagan as a Deputy Assistant Secretary of Defense, and was well aware of the implications of disobeying an order. But he also understood the implications of forcing Americans to wear a foreign uniform.

I called Colonel Ray. He asked for a few days to check out the story. He called back and said, "I'll take the case." We had not discussed money so I brought the issue up, "We don't have any money to pay you." "I didn't ask you for any money," he replied. "This case is about the sovereignty of the United States of America." "I appreciate your patriotism," I replied, "but this is going to take a lot of time and money to fight. If people want to help, I want to send you some money." Colonel Ray said, "That's fine. If people donate money, you send it. But we can't let the lack of money prevent this case from being fought in the proper way."

Following that conversation, we began a whirlwind of activity, traveling to Kentucky and setting up a Defense Fund. Ron Ray and his wife, Eunice, worked countless hours during that first year, alongside our own family, getting the story out and preparing for the court martial. Colonel Ray put together a legal team to fight the case on both military and civilian fronts.

Both Ron and I did hundreds of media interviews on the subject. In an interview with the Washington Post, Ron was asked to counter claims by some that Michael was given an order that he disobeyed and that he had to be punished for it. "It is a crime in the military to show up for duty out of uniform," Ron told the paper. "People are routinely prosecuted for putting on decorations they didn't earn." This was precisely the point: Michael was given an illegal order to wear a foreign uniform. He could not legally or morally comply.

Even though Col. Ray has since returned to his private practice, we have continued to use the legal team that he helped us put together through five court appearances over the past three years. For the court-martial, we needed someone with specific Army experience. We were fortunate to find Henry Hamilton, retired lieutenant-colonel in the Army's Judicial

Advisory Group, now a private attorney in Columbia, South Carolina. "Hank" Hamilton had actually served in Germany for the final years of his career, knew the layout, knew the individuals involved in the prosecution, and has done a wonderful job in meeting the Army requirements of the case. We also accepted the *pro-bono* offer of Michael Farris on the civilian side of the case. Mike is a Virginia attorney, founder and head of the Home School Legal Defense Association, and a former candidate for lieutenant governor in Virginia. This team will continue to evolve as conditions change, but each individual has made a valuable contribution both to our family and the protection of constitutional rights in this country.

Convinced that the law, the Constitution and military regulations are all on his side, Mike Farris believes that Michael will eventually win the case if it gets decided on the merits. "This is not a case of a soldier refusing to peel potatoes," he points out. Indeed, this is a case of a solder who refused to follow orders that contradicted his sacred oath, the law, the Constitution and military regulations.

I'm proud of my son. I wish I were as proud of my government.

Chapter 2

"Obey God, Serve Mankind, Oppose Tyranny"

★ ★ ★ ★

"The best way to have peace is to always be prepared to fight a war."

—*George Washington*

Michael New will go down in American history as the first American soldier to refuse to wear the United Nations uniform. He will not be the last. We pray that his example will serve to educate other soldiers about the stakes involved, and that they will take appropriate action.

In Michael's case, I have been asked on many occasions, "Did you influence your son to do this or did he do it by himself?" My answer is "Yes," and, "Yes."

I should hope that, as his father, I influenced my son. (It's almost a reflection of what this nation has become that such a question is asked.) After all, my grandfather taught my father, my father taught me, and I taught my son. We were all taught to serve our country. Members of our family have served in every American war, dating back to the first American War for Independence.[1] It's a proud tradition. It's the American way. Great Americans gave their all to bring our nation into existence, and further sacrifices have maintained our national independence and security. All of this is now at risk.

At the same time, having been taught to think for himself, Michael New did not call home and ask what to do. Instead, he called us and told us of the decision he had made and that his objection was already lodged with his chain of command. Anyone who knows our children knows that they are not pup-

[1] There has been no declared American war since 1941. That is to say, there has been no legal American war since that date.

pets or wimps unable to think for themselves.

The chapters in this book are designed to educate the American people about how our sovereignty is being eroded, and what steps can be taken to reverse course. But let's face it: it's imperative that the next generation understand these lessons as well. Since we somehow instilled in Michael a fundamental appreciation of America's unique contribution to world history, many have asked me how he turned out this way. Was there a "secret" in raising a young man in this fashion?

There's nothing secret about it. Suzanne and I raised our three sons, Michael, Gabriel and Gamaliel, along with their four sisters, Kyria Rae, Rebecca, Rachel and Halcyon, to expect to serve our fellow man and our country.

This doesn't necessarily mean that a young man or woman has to go into military service. But when Michael joined the Army in 1993, we understood the implications. We both recognized that he might be required to give his life. We understood that. He understood that. We believe these things are fundamental to a strong nation – a willingness to serve.

We regard it as a God-given responsibility to defend one's family and one's country.[2] It is no privilege to die in service to some country that hates us or our values, nor to serve a governmental power that is inherently anti-Christian. The United Nations is anti-Christian. This is irrefutable.

The decision to join the service was a momentous one. And the military, with its good order and discipline, was expected to be an extremely positive experience. He worked very hard to be a good soldier. He was decorated for meritorious service, including the saving of lives on maneuvers.

But whether Michael had joined the military or had gone into the private civilian sector, we had the same high expectations of him. We expected him to serve, to set high standards and be an example to others, to do what is right, and to fear

---

[2] As long as a country serves its citizens by protecting their freedoms, in particular the freedom to worship as we choose. We don't regard it as a duty to serve a power that is anti-Christian – in fact, we consider it impossible for a Christian to do so in good faith.

God. Suzanne and I prayed virtually every single day that Michael would be, "a bright light in a dark place." We had no idea how bright a light, nor how dark a place it would be. We never anticipated that Michael would have to take his stand inside the military, and that the military establishment, under the administration of President Bill Clinton, would come down on him like a ton of bricks.

Michael's view – and our view – has frequently been distorted by the press. I was asked at one point what I thought about Michael becoming a "cause celebre for isolationism." But our position has never been isolationist. In fact, we think America should strive to export Freedom around the world. America once stood as a shining example to other nations. We simply believe in the sovereignty of our country. And we're still trying to figure out when, and how, that became a crime.

We believe that America ought to further American national interests, not those of the U.N. or the rest of the world. We are just ethnocentric enough to think that America, in many ways, really is superior to most other countries, in spite of its many imperfections. We believe our faith in God is something other countries need. And before they can assume the façade of a republican form of government, they must first build a foundation which we believe comes straight out of the Bible. As I've said in many speeches around the country, the "Cradle of Liberty is not Lexington and Concord Bridge. It is the preceding 150 years of fathers reading the Bible to their children every morning and every evening." These views, which are not universal today in America, were universal at the founding of our country.

Michael himself was prepared to serve the U.S. military and American interests in any country. Indeed, he even served in a U.N.-authorized (American-led) military operation in the Persian Gulf after the conclusion of the Gulf War. He didn't like it, and neither did we. But a soldier does not have the privilege of "picking and choosing" the orders he wants to obey. Michael's personal "line in the sand" came when he was told he would have to serve U.N. interests in a U.N. uniform under a UN commanding general.

There are those who believe that Michael took his stand against the U.N. because he had lived a sheltered existence and was isolated from the outside world. Nothing could be further from the truth. Michael was very much exposed to the outside world, far more than most kids. As missionaries, we lived and worked in Papua New Guinea, in New Zealand, and in The Philippines. He was exposed to many different cultures and peoples. He speaks fluent Tagalog and used to speak Tokpisin of PNG. In fact, it was because of the foreign culture exposure we were experiencing that it became even more of a responsibility for us to instill in our children an idea or concept of what it meant to be an American.

Home Schooling

It was during this period of time, when our children were in their most formative years, that we found ourselves home schooling them out of necessity. Home schooling involves an informal learning atmosphere between parents and children that may not be appropriate for everyone. Some parents are happy with the education their children are getting from government, private or parochial schools. But home school really fits our lifestyle and our value system. We found that home schooling facilitates the ability to teach the values we share, and to communicate them to our children, and we don't have to spend a lot of time deprogramming them daily from the social engineering going on in all governments schools today.[3]

It's interesting to note that Michael Farris, president of the Home School Legal Defense Association (HSLDA), has

---

[3] Lest I'm ambiguous here, you may read "social engineering" as "Marxist garbage." But lest I offend one of those wonderful teachers who is still in the system, resisting the meltdown that every teacher over the past forty years has witnessed, let me hasten to say that we admire missionaries, and regard a good teacher with Biblical values as a true missionary. No continent has ever been darker than our own government school system. Many children today don't even know what the Ten Commandments are. Some of these teachers are my heroes. But my children are not available to be sacrificed on the altar to Darwin and Dewey that our government schools have become today.

taken on one of Michael's court cases for several reasons, including the belief that the U.N. represents a threat to the growing home schooling movement. He points out that the U.N. has been trying to gain control over our families through intrusive international agreements such as the U.N. Convention on the Rights of the Child.

Home schooling is growing. In 1983, HSLDA had 837 member-families. By 1998, that had grown to 58,000 families. Currently, over 1.5 million children are being home-schooled in this country. It's good for students spiritually and educationally.[4] The future leadership for Freedom will come from these students. No doubt, the future leadership for the "Brave New World" predicted by Aldous Huxley will come from the "government schools."[5] Discerning American parents are waking up and realizing that the brainwashing taking place in government schools is carefully calculated to bring about a student that does not share the values of his or her parents.[6] Unfortunately, most of us wake up too late to repair the damage. Worse yet, many never figure out where the attack on our values is coming from.

In spite of the many wonderful Christian teachers who daily try to help their students, the situation has become poi-

[4] Homeschoolers, on the whole, perform better on tests than children who attend government schools. Just as important, if not more, they are being taught values that makes them individuals, able to think for themselves instead of becoming little automatons, each programmed with the latest trend in politically correct thinking. Outcome Based Education cannot reach homeschoolers, and that is one of two reasons why the National Education Association and the Educrats of this nation are determined to destroy it by any means possible. The other, obviously, is money. Government schools today seem incapable of educating children, even with a budget of $6,000 or more per student. But they still resent the loss of income that home schooled student represents. A home schooling mother with a budget of $250 can do a better job, on average.

[5] The first Humanist Manifesto was published in 1933. Co-author John Dewey, the noted philosopher and educator, calls for a synthesizing of all religions and "a socialized and cooperative economic order." Co-signer C.F. Potter said in 1930, "Education is thus a most powerful ally of humanism, and every American public school is a school of humanism. What can the theistic Sunday schools, meeting for an hour once a week, teaching only a fraction of the children, do to stem the tide of a five-day program of humanistic teaching?" Source: Dr. Dennis Cuddy.

[6] "Rather than adding my voice to those who urge us to go 'back to basics' I would argue that we need to move ahead to the new basics...the arts of compromise and reconciliation, of consensus building, and of planning for interdependence, a command of these talents becomes 'basic'...As young people mature, we must help them develop...the global servant concept in which we will educate our young for planetary service and eventually for some form of world citizenship."—Sept. 1976, Phi Delta Kappa printed "America's Next 25 Years: Some Implications for Education," by Harold Shane, Project Director for the NEA Bicentennial Committee.

soned with socialist planners above, and a humanist curriculum in their hands, so that the teacher who tries to offset the system has become, indeed, a missionary to the dark continent of government schools.[7] Only one quote to substantiate this claim will I put in the main text. The rest will appear among the footnotes.

> "Among the elementary measures the American Soviet government will adopt to further the Cultural Revolution are... [a] National Department of Education... the studies will be revolutionized, being cleansed of religious, patriotic, and other features of the bourgeois ideology. The students will be taught the basis of Marxian dialectical materialism, internationalism and the general ethics of the new Socialist society."[8]

Is this not precisely what is being taught more children in today's government schools? Just as Foster predicted, they are taught "dialectical materialism" (based upon Darwin and Marx) in all science, all social studies classes, and in literature - in fact it's virtually against the law to mention the Faith of our Founding Fathers. When that subject does come up, it's usually to mock them and castigate them at every opportunity. They are taught internationalism at every corner, while pride of our own nation is reduced. Top students no longer go to model legislatures for exercises in civics, but to Model United Nations workshops in most states! And of course, the "general ethics of the new Socialist Society" are permeated

[7] "Every child in America entering school at the age of five is mentally ill because he comes to school with certain allegiances to our founding fathers, toward our elected officials, toward his parents, toward a belief in a supernatural being, and toward the sovereignty of this nation as a separate entity. It is up to you as teachers to make all of these sick children well — by creating the international child of the future."— Dr. Chester M. Pierce, Professor of Education at Harvard, addressing the Association for Childhood Education International in April, 1972. Quoted by Ruth Love in 'Drawing Line on Freedom-Abuse,' Lebanon News, April, 1985. Also by Bruce Wiseman, in his article, 'Educational and Social Ruin,' in Destroying Lives, Psychiatry Education's Ruin, as published by the Citizens Commission on Human Rights, 1995. CCHR International, 6362 Hollywood Blvd., Suite B, Los Angeles, CA 90028

[8] William Z. Foster, Toward Soviet America, 1932. When one studies this issue and the literature published from Karl Marx to John Dewey to the various Marxist and Socialist 'revolutionary educators' of the twenties and thirties, and compares them to the books and articles coming to your local school system via the NEA today, there is clearly an ideological trail that can be established. The documentation is complete to any who wish to review it, but it ís outside the scope of this book.

throughout the "Outcome Based Education," " Goals 2000," and "School to Work" projects to be found in virtually every government school in America. Coincidence? I don't think so.

Perhaps it was an error that we taught our children very little about the United Nations, but we have tended to focus instead on teaching them to love their country, and to understand where these blessings of Freedom come from. So, when Michael compared the U.S. Constitution to the U.N. Charter, he understood the differences. This lesson in world politics, urged on him by his military superiors, reinforced the pro-American sentiments we had instilled in him. For many soldiers, the outcome might not have been so welcome. Michael himself points out that soldiers in basic training are given very little, if any, appreciation of constitutional rights, obligations and provisions as they relate to the military.

This makes it even more urgent that we, as parents, instill these values in our young people. If there's a secret, this is it. Students certainly aren't getting this emphasis in government schools. Nor are churches instilling patriotic values. The "separation of Church and State" issue has been abused and misused in a way that would astonish our Founding Fathers. With the State unable to benefit from the moral influence of the Church, and with the Church avoiding good citizenship as "political," both have suffered immensely.

In our view, parenting has become a lost art, partly due to the mobility of people today and the "globalization" of the economy that has forced millions of women and young mothers into the work force to meet the financial needs of their families. As this trend continues, there will be additional pressure on families to rely on schools or day-care centers for education and care of their children. Despite these pressures, we believe that parents have to find the time to spend with their children to make sure they grow up with an appreciation of America's Christian heritage.

In our case, Suzanne does most of the day-to-day teaching. I focus on social studies and government, and outdoor skills and projects, along with curriculum planning. After the first year we found that we liked the ability to select texts and workbooks from different companies, and even from used bookstores, where many great textbooks and history books are gathering dust. Curriculum doesn't have to be expensive.

Suzanne and I always felt it was incumbent on us to instill in our children a mindset of respect and honor, both for parents and for the Founding Fathers, who risked their lives, their fortunes, and their sacred honor to bestow the blessings of liberty to us, their posterity. The "Literature of Liberty," including America's founding documents, was an important part of my family's library as I was growing up, and continues to be a central part of the curricula that our children read today. For that I have my own parents to thank.

The heroes of the American War of Independence were inspirational to me. In addition, I grew up with an appreciation of patriots such as William Wallace, the Scottish hero portrayed in the recent movie, "Braveheart." William Tell stirred me over and over with his refusal to bow to a symbol of tyranny. We're convinced that this is the sort of literature parents ought to be looking for as they attempt to instill an appreciation of Freedom in their children.

The Scots in William Wallace's day had a very strong sense of right and wrong, and of liberty. But they had corrupt leaders who made deals with the enemy, who betrayed their national sovereignty, and who considered personal gain more important than their responsibility to lead their people. They had made tactical and strategic alliances with the English to maintain their own positions of power and prestige and to gain territory. In return, they had compromised and lost their freedom. Today, we are losing our freedom, our country, our national identity as a people, as well as our Christian heritage.

I believe Michael was following in the footsteps of William Wallace as well as those of our own Founders. Of course, Michael was not required to sacrifice his life, only his military career. But he was prepared, if necessary, to go to prison, and really without complaint. As he said at the time, "A lot of people have gone to prison for what they believed in. I'd be in good company." Later, only half in jest, he said, "I was prepared to go prison, but I wasn't prepared to be famous." The attention, the cameras, and the interviews have been overwhelming.

Michael New is not a person who acts in order to be appreciated. He knows who he is and is secure in that knowledge. He doesn't seek the approval of the crowd. In fact, it has been painful to him to have standing ovations for him for simply doing his duty. For that reason, he no longer accepts speaking engagements, stating simply, "Actions speak louder than words. I've acted. Others may talk about it." He continues to stand up where it counts – in a court of law. He may lose every round, but we are convinced that we are right, and must not be intimidated at the odds, any more than the Founding Fathers were.

In order to appreciate Michael's stand for America and recapture the spirit of this great country, we must re-educate our young people, teaching them about the principles of self-government and God-given rights that are embedded in our Declaration of Independence, the U.S. Constitution, and the Bill of Rights. John Paul Jones, Paul Revere, Nathan Hale and Patrick Henry are not just names. They are heroic figures whose contributions to American history have to be conveyed to our children and grandchildren. Our schools, our entertainment media, and television are not doing that.

We taught our children that the U.S is based on a Constitution penned by men who believed in God, a Divine Creator who gave us certain unalienable rights – rights which cannot be lawfully taken away by any government. This is the critical difference between the American philosophy and the U.N. philosophy. Our Declaration of Independence declares openly that our rights come from God. The U.N. Charter, by contrast, makes no reference to a Creator, nor can it, since it was organized and has been run ever since by atheists who believe there is only one higher thing than the evolved human, and that is the Collective. The individual has no rights that might interfere with the "Human Rights" of "the People." This kind of rhetoric is right out of Marx and Lenin.

One of many examples of this comes from President Clinton's recent visit to Communist China, where he gave a speech at Beijing University and was praised by some for emphasizing human rights and standing up to the Communists. There was a glaring omission in Clinton's speech when he failed to mention government-sanctioned infanticide, forced abortion and sterilization, slave labor, and many other abuses of Freedom in Red China.

Instead, his performance included praise for the Communist bosses in Beijing having brought the "liberty" of "economic security" to many Chinese people. Clinton said "economic security" was "an essential element of freedom" because it "is recognized in the United Nations Covenant on Economic, Social and Cultural Rights."

However, no such "right" is found in the Constitution or the Declaration of Independence. Economic security is one of those so-called "rights" which matters to socialist or communist governments which want to plan the economy and control peoples' lives and property. The former Soviet regime also claimed that it had provided "economic security" to its Soviet people. This notion of "economic security" is actually a smokescreen for denying freedom to subjects who are regarded as dangerous for wanting the freedom of self-determination.

Clinton's reference to the Chinese authorities giving their people "economic security" was a form of pandering. An analysis of his speech shows that he devoted significantly more time and attention to U.N. treaties than the U.S. Constitution and the Declaration of Independence.

Rather than emphasize the unique nature of America's founding documents and the recognition that human rights come from God, Clinton said that certain rights were "universal" and "enshrined in the United Nations Declaration on Human Rights." He said they were not uniquely American. One treaty Clinton did not mention was the Convention on the Elimination of All Forms of Discrimination Against Women, which is supposed to guarantee women's rights. China has signed the treaty and claims to be in compliance, but its one-child per family policy proves that is a big lie.

It was noteworthy that Clinton referred to human rights being "universal," whatever that means, rather than God-given. This reveals his real philosophy of life.

Ironically, as Clinton was traveling in China and downplaying our founding as a Christian nation, the Library of Congress was sponsoring an exhibit called "Religion and the Founding of the American Republic." Librarian of Congress James Billington unveiled the exhibit, saying, "The dominant role religion played in the earliest days of this country is largely ignored by media, academics and others." These comments did not make front-page news. Rather, they ended up in a story on page nine of the second section of the Washington Post. The Post, of course, is a very secular paper which treats Christmas as a holiday featuring Santa Claus rather than Jesus Christ. Still, the decision to play down James Billington's comments is extraordinary. To my knowledge, Billington is not a member of the Christian Coalition. Yet here he was making a statement about religion, public life and the media that could have come from the lips of a conservative Christian.

The Post story about the exhibit carried the subheadline, "Library of Congress Looks at a Cozier Era in Church-State

Relations." Consider that phrase "cozier era." This is how the Post acknowledges that the founding fathers envisioned a close relationship between religion and public life. The Post actually reproduced the Liberty Window, from Christ Church in Philadelphia, which depicted the Continental Congress praying in 1774. Some of them were on their knees.

The Congress is still opened with a prayer every day, but can you imagine a majority of its members praying on their knees as C-SPAN cameras capture the event? How America has changed. But why have we changed? As Billington suggests, it is clear that things have changed because the media and other important elements in society have developed a bias against the celebration of religious values. The surveys show that very few members of the Washington media even attend church.

The Post story about the Library of Congress exhibit notes that it includes a letter President Thomas Jefferson wrote in 1802 to the Dansbury Baptist Association in Connecticut. This is the letter in which the famous phrase "separation of church and state" appears. The Post noted that the phrase has been cited in several Supreme Court decisions since the 1870s that attempt to make sense of the First Amendment. Today, the phrase is quoted as if it were actually part of the Constitution.

What the Post does not make clear is the time-line — that Jefferson's phrase "separation of church and state" was written 13 years after the First Amendment was ratified. What's more, Jefferson did not write the First Amendment and was not even in the country when the Constitution was written. And the bottom line on Jefferson's famous phrase is that he was addressing the issue of the government interfering with churches, and not the other way around.

A better judge of the meaning of the First Amendment was George Washington, president of the Continental Congress and President of the country when the First Amendment was passed and ratified. Washington is one of those leaders depicted in the Liberty Window kneeling and praying to God.

Suzanne and I have tried to pass on to our children an appreciation for America's founding documents and a hunger for learning. At age 11, I remember asking my own father to explain to me the difference between freedom and communism in terms I could understand. This gave rise to an emerging philosophy or worldview that Suzanne and I, in turn, would convey to all our children. I became an avid student of the "literature of freedom," and my parents supplied me with what seemed like an endless supply of materials explaining the founding and history of America. Michael shared this enthusiasm. All of our seven children became avid readers.

My father, who served in the Marine Corp in World War II,[9] reminded me of a letter I had sent to him from The Philippines some years ago. In that letter, I told my father about how pleased I was that Michael had asked me, at age 13, to "teach me more about the Declaration of Independence and the Constitution..." This is the hunger for truth that we must convey to the next generation. We must pass it on through example. We should read with our children, from our founding documents and the Bible.

I remember, while living in The Philippines, teaching the older children about feudalism, a legal and political system in which the people are servants of a ruling class. The people under feudalism were known as vassals. The term "vassal state" grew out of this, to signify those countries which become subservient to larger powers. I remember telling them that serving those rulers also entailed being part of their armies at the beck and call of one's "lord." I told them that anytime you could take the armed forces of one country and place them under the control of a foreign power, that country is not, by definition, a free country.

In order to make this more relevant to our young people, we believe it is helpful and educational to trace family back-

[9] Communications, Company H, 2nd Battalion, 22nd Regiment, which was later attached to the 6th Marine Division.

grounds and history. Many of us can trace our backgrounds to ancestors who came to America to escape persecution and find freedom. Educating our young people about this history can open them up to a fruitful discussion of how all of this is now at risk because of our deepening involvement with the U.N.

Another important exercise can be coming up with a work-able family motto – one that reflects your values. Together, as a school exercise, we developed one for our family:

> **Obey God,**
>
> **Serve Mankind,**
>
> **Oppose Tyranny.**

A motto can, on occasion, capture a whole philosophy of life, and it can stick with a young person throughout his or her life.[10]

The phrase "Obey God" is undoubtedly the most profound part of that motto. No one can serve two masters. We truly believe that, in refusing to serve the U.N., Michael was being obedient to his conscience to obey God first and only. He was speaking and acting as a Christian young man.

Another lesson we taught Michael was to resist peer pres-sure. We taught him that what the rest of the crowd does has nothing to do with what is right. This lesson was important when Michael made that fateful decision not to wear the U.N. uniform and fall into formation. He was scorned and ridiculed. They tried to embarrass him. It would have been so easy for him to simply give up and join the crowd. Today we laugh when we consider the occasional charge that Michael was a coward who was afraid to deploy. I challenge anyone to deliberately choose his path and stick it out and see what they're made of. It was not the easy path.

He was given another chance to "wise up" and put on the U.N. uniform, but he refused, despite the pressure. He did what was right. And for that, we remain grateful and proud. God has blessed us. God has blessed Michael. God bless America.

---

[10] Mary Rutkowski of Idaho recently supplied the Latin translation: *"Veremini Deum, Servite Homines, Obsistite Tyrannidem."*

America Responds to the News

How Americans learned about Michael New, and what he had done, remains an incredible story in and of itself, and I pray the reader will indulge me here, or else skip on to the next chapter.

After Mike's phone call from Germany, we were more than a little anxious about the implications of what he had done and where we might turn for help. I told Suzanne what had happened and we prayed.

I sat at my desk in my office, and began to articulate just exactly what qualifications did a person need to have in order for them to be able to give us some advice. I concluded that we needed someone who (a) had a military background; (b) had legal expertise; and (c) was not afraid to disagree with the federal government. Almost as I finished that short list, the radio announced, "Stay tuned for G. Gordon Liddy!" Was that an answer to prayer? I don't know, but Liddy certainly met the requirements. I picked up the phone and dialed the toll-free number, and like a miracle, I was the first caller through that morning! At this point I was beginning to suspect that I really did have Divine Intervention, because it's virtually impossible to get on those programs, not to mention being the first caller, first try.

Mr. Liddy listened and gave us some advice we took very seriously. He said, "My guess is that you're not made of money, so I'll advise you now to have your son take his licks and get out of the Army and come home and get a real job and get on with his life." That wasn't encouraging, but then he said, "On the other hand, this is clearly a threshold case. It may well be that if you fight it, and if you somehow find a way to fund that fight, you just may well change the course of American history." As a caution, he added, "Don't start a fight you aren't prepared to finish, win or lose." We will always be grateful for the common sense G. Gordon Liddy instilled into our thinking from the beginning, along with the encouraging words that this case is one of historic proportions.

Within an hour I sent a message via e-mail to a good friend, Joe Sager, who played around with a private electronic bulletin board. I told Joe that Michael seemed to have a problem, that he might well be court-martialed for refusing to wear a United Nations helmet, and that if Joe had any advise for Mike, he might like to send it to him in Germany. I included Michael's APO address for Germany.

About three days later I came back to my computer to check my mail, which would normally have ten to twenty messages in three days. Imagine my surprise to find over 300 messages waiting on me! As I watched them come down, I thought the bulletin board computer had gone haywire.

Instead, Joe had put my message on the internet for any and all to read, and this was the first response. Many told me they had already written to Michael, written to their congressman, written to their editors, etc., and wasn't there more they could do?

This was around Thursday or Friday, and I felt obligated to get hold of Michael and warn him that some mail was on the way. We had to go through the Red Cross, but we finally found him. I told him he'd be getting some mail on Saturday, and he said, "No, I won't." Why not? "Because they don't deliver mail on Saturday."

"Oh. Alright," I said, "then you'll be getting some mail on Monday." (I didn't want to scare him with numbers, just "some mail.")

Again he said, "No, I won't." Why not? "Because Monday is Labor Day. No mail."

"Alright, wise guy," I was exasperated now, "whenever the mail does come, you're going to get some, and don't blame me, blame Joe Sager."

We waited through the weekend, and through Labor Day, for Mike to call on Tuesday. "You were right," he said, "I did get some mail."

"How much?"

"I don't know."

"Why not?"

"I didn't count it."

"Why not?" I think the exasperation may have been coming through at this point.

"Because I've been busy reading it. Look, I was carrying the second big mail bag of mail from the mail room to my quarters, and I was dropping stuff, and the sergeant came along and wanted to know what I was doing, besides littering up the place." At this point I was beginning to get a picture. "I really don't know how much mail I got," he continued, but he later estimated it at around 1,500 pieces of mail.

Over the following weeks he received thousands more, and the same people were calling and faxing both Congress and one another, telling them of his plight.

While the Media sat on the story

Did you initially read about this story in your local newspaper? Probably not. Even though we gave the story to a local reporter in Conroe, Texas, who filed it with Associated Press immediately, in Dallas, it was not released for weeks. They sat on the story. Apparently it didn't meet the politically correct slant that AP looks for in a story. No sex, no oppressed minority, no gender conflict, etc. Simply a story of an American standing up for the sovereignty of the nation. Ho, hum.

But Americans weren't bored with the story. Our phone began to ring. Radio talk show hosts wanted the story. Where did they learn about it? From listeners who called them. There's a poor fellow in Houston, Texas, a painter by the name of Daniel New (probably a distant relative), who got about a jillion calls and who was gracious enough to pass on our number to most of them. We began to do interviews with anyone who would call us. We didn't have time to pursue interviews.

Perhaps the largest show, early on, was the Chuck Harder show. It was instrumental in spreading the word far and wide. There were several syndicated shows, and several on short-wave, which gave nation-wide coverage. We finally quit counting but in the past three years we've done over 1,500 interviews. It was fun at first, but we're grateful that the pace has slowed down.

The first nationwide periodical to interview Michael was *The New American*. William Norman Grigg interviewed him by phone in Germany and got right on the story. They came out with a cover-page article that sounded the alarm to all their readers. Right behind them was *The Spotlight*, which publishes weekly and, as a result, managed to get their story into print first. Their front-page story helped stir up even more support. We are grateful for those and all coverage, both objective and sympathetic. I must, in all fairness, mention that the Houston Chronicle and the television and radio stations around Houston gave the story great coverage.

Part of the story, of course, is why the mainstream media steadfastly refused, then and now, to give this story the time of day, while devoting hundreds of column inches to Kelly Flynn and Shannon Faulkner, both of whom were "politically correct."

When Carla Robbins, of the *Wall Street Journal*, came to Texas to cover my campaign for Congress, she repeatedly asked me, "Where is the media on this story?"

I had to laugh. "Carla, you're the reporter, you tell me." I found it as humorous as she found it mystifying that, whether or not we agreed with Michael's position, it was a newsworthy story. I also found it interesting that a liberal reporter, a member of the Council on Foreign Relations, who disagreed with almost every position we held, could write an article which was an objective work of journalism. I'm grateful to the editors of the *Wall Street Journal* for their coverage and the front-page placement of the article. It was a notable exception.

From time to time, of course, some newspaper would run an article, and I could tell because my phone would start ringing. When the story broke in Oklahoma City it was a Sunday, I recall, and our phone rang all day long. Every one of those people who found us had to go to the trouble of going through an information operator.

When the story broke in Chicago it was the *Sun Times* which carried it on page 1-A, along with a reader poll asking people their opinion. A few days later they published the results – 83% of Chicagoans agreed with Michael! The story suddenly disappeared from print in Chicago, as if it had never happened.

The amusing and interesting thing about this is that newspaper and television voices continually lament their own decline and publicly ponder, "What happened?" The conventional answer is that technology is passing them by, and they will go the way of the papyrus & quill, the clay tablet & stylus. There's an element of truth to that. But the role of mainstream media has been highly managed, highly filtered, and highly controlled by a media elite for decades. Now they cannot understand why the public is ignoring them as we find new and better ways to get more information without the spin they've traditionally given us. The refusal by the major traditional news sources to give us honest journalism when they had a lock on it, has resulted in their being abandoned by many people today without a sigh of remorse.

An example of this is the recent criticism of Matt Drudge and the Drudge report, where mainstream journalists are whining about his success and how there need to be "filters" to protect the people from raw information. Raw information is truth, and no journalist should fear the people learning the truth. On the other hand, every tyrant is afraid of an uncontrolled media.

While on the air in various communities around the country, I've had callers tell me, "Today I sent 300 fax messages to my friends all over the country. What else can I do?" This sort of "samizdat"[11] journalism via fax and e-mail is changing the way politicians and bureaucrats have to do business, because stories can no longer be buried the way they used to be.

In the meantime, certain columnists have established themselves as valuable commodities, offering insight and analysis to readers who might otherwise miss the stories, or who haven't read between the lines and seen a particular angle. Charley Reese of the *Orlando Sentinel*, Dr. Dennis Cuddy, an independent writer, and Samuel Francis, then of the *Washington Times*, all three wrote outstanding columns which are available in the appendices of this book. Cliff Kincaid's coverage was also worth mentioning, with articles in the American Legion monthly magazine and others.

Newspapers and other mainstream media such as television and radio have reduced themselves to nothing more than a collective medium of advertising and entertainment. They are no longer about "news." They've done it to themselves, and they deserve what happens to them.

All in all, the ability of Americans to get information quickly has undergone, and is undergoing, such a revolution that it offers tremendous possibilities in upsetting the status quo for those who have maintained power through keeping the populace ignorant for as long a period as possible. If knowledge is power, then the loss of control over information offers power back to the People, at the expense of the Elite who have had it their way for too long.

---

[11] *Samizdat* – the underground newspapers of the Soviet Union kept people informed of facts and of developments that the official press would never cover.

Chapter 3

Resistance to Illegal Orders
★★★★

"If ye love wealth better than liberty, the tranquility of servitude better than the animating contest of freedom, go home from us in peace.
We ask not your counsels or arms. Crouch down and lick the hands which feed you. May your chains set lightly upon you, and may posterity forget ye were our countrymen."
—Samuel Adams

Moved by Michael's stand, Americans have sent more than just letters of support. Many have told of their own experiences in the military, or other bureaucracies, and how they stood alone. It has made for inspiring reading.

Hundreds have sent books and articles, documenting the growth of the coming One World Government known as the United Nations. They've also documented some of the many warnings over the past fifty years from various voices who have been warning the American public that national sovereignty and international authority are mutually exclusive concepts.[1]

Those voices have correctly pointed to the historical record that once a nation surrenders any portion of its sovereignty, it is virtually impossible to regain it. In the past decade the number of voices has increased. The mainstream press has maintained a steady silence on the subject.

Michael's stand for American sovereignty, which by necessity placed him in a position against the United Nations, and therefore against our own official national security policy, would not have been possible without the support of the many soldiers and veterans who recognized the validity of his cause.

---

[1] See the Bibliography for a listing of a few of them.

Literally thousands have come forward in his support. As this case continues to unfold, we want to extend an invitation to more of them to take a stand. It is not too late. Indeed, the United States of America will not survive as an independent nation unless many more Americans stand up and defend her sovereignty.

Major Charles Johnson, USMC, (res.)

Immediately after learning about Michael's position, I began to call friends and friends of friends, looking for advice. Someone gave me the name of Chuck Johnson, of Wisconsin. I dialed the number, got no answer, and decided it was another dead end. But a few days later my phone rang and Johnson had heard the story and decided to call me.

I learned that Chuck Johnson had given up a career in the Marine Corps, over his intense disagreement with President Clinton's policy of allowing homosexuals to serve in the military. Spurning a pension, and with a family to feed, he instead walked away from a career that was only a couple of years away from retirement.

Major Charles Johnson, (Resigned), is an American hero. Like most real heroes, he won't let me call him that to his face. But he represents what makes, or rather made, America great. Johnson's advice to me was to call a friend of his, Ronald Ray of Kentucky. I did. It was a life-altering phone call.

Colonel Ronald D. Ray, USMC, (ret.)

Ron Ray is a retired Marine Colonel and a highly decorated Vietnam veteran, who served under Ronald Reagan as Deputy Assistant Secretary of Defense in the Pentagon. He understands how "the system" works. Ray deserves special credit for immediately recognizing the implications of the case, and accepting the challenge of crafting a legal defense.

From the beginning, our phones began to ring with requests that we discuss the case on local radio talk shows and even on some larger syndicated shows. Colonel Ray and I took to the airwaves to articulate to a national audience why the Clinton Administration's pro-U.N. policy was unlawful and unconstitutional. He said the process of building a case against the administration amounted to "breaking the code," a reference to the administration's use of a paper trail that attempted to obscure the fact that there was no legal or constitutional basis for the Macedonia deployment.

From the viewpoint of a human being and a combat veteran, Colonel Ray talked about how Michael New had consistently failed to get a satisfactory answer to a very basic question: "By what authority do you order me to wear a United Nations uniform?" He points out that, as a soldier, Michael "had a duty" to ask the question and yet, to this day, it has never been "substantively answered."

The reason, of course, is that the policy has not been implemented in accordance with the Constitution, nor with statutory law, nor with Defense Department and Army regulations. "The reason they didn't answer it is that *there is no authority*," Colonel Ray explains.

Nevertheless, because he merely asked the question, Michael "was threatened with jail, a court-martial and a less than honorable discharge." The Army tried "to coerce, intimidate, and to move Michael into compliance," Ray said.

Explaining the significance of the case at a press conference in Germany, Colonel Ray stated, "No soldier in American history has ever been charged with a crime for questioning the wearing of a foreign badge, a foreign insignia, a foreign uniform, much less court-martialed and convicted and given a Bad Conduct Discharge. This is an historic case." Ray called the response to Michael New an indication of how "compromised" the Army has become, "the degree to which our military is willing to accommodate political pressures which do not stand constitutional or legal scrutiny."

David S. Sullivan, LTC, USMC (ret.)

Colonel Ray's associate, David Sullivan, did much of the original research into the case which conclusively demonstrated the legal and constitutional bankruptcy of Clinton's pro-U.N. policy.

Dave, a former CIA analyst and senior Congressional staffer who is also a decorated combat veteran of the Vietnam War, discussed the actual transformation of U.S. troops into U.N. personnel through the requirement that they carry U.N. identity cards. This means they lose their status as American soldiers and American POWs if captured. With tears forming in his eyes, Dave has explained this issue in very personal terms, noting that his own father was missing in action for some time during World War II. "It's a very emotional issue for all Americans," he points out.

The issue of U.N. I.D. has major ramifications. American troops carry American Armed Forces identification cards which entitle them to certain international rights and protections under the Geneva Conventions on War of 1949. In Vietnam, of course, the Communists did not live up to these standards, and the U.S. was reluctant to invoke the treaty to protect its POWs. Nevertheless, the Geneva Convention is a "thread of hope" for all U.S. troops.

Referring to reports that soldiers are now being required to give DNA samples to the military so the government can "identify the pieces of you if you come back" from a war, Dave Sullivan points out: "However, they're not so concerned about your live body because they're willing to transform you, in violation of your oath of office as a member of the Armed Forces and in violation of your oath to the Constitution, into a United Nations soldier."

In Michael New's case, the Army has reluctantly admitted that the U.N. uniform for U.S. troops is required under "U.N. guidelines", not the U.S. Constitution, and that the uniform includes a U.N. cap, beret or helmet, hat badge, cloth soldier patch, armlet and scarf. The guidelines also said, "While in transit to and from the mission area, contingent personnel must be in possession of identification in accordance with their national regulations. On arrival [in the assigned theatre of operations], personnel will be issued a U.N. peacekeeping force identification card which will be the only identify document required within the area of operation."

The Army has made a big deal out of refuting our contention that "American soldiers must give up their American ID," claiming that we have misrepresented the case to the American public. While it's true that we did say that in an early press release, (because that's what we were told), we quickly corrected it in all subsequent releases, and have been careful to stick to the facts. But the Army, in the meantime, has been misinforming Congressional offices throughout this entire legal battle with this story, hammering on our mistake, and in the process, obfuscating the entire issue. This has been a deliberate distortion of the truth.

In this case, American soldiers become "U.N. troops" and are given "protection" under a meaningless, unenforceable "Convention on Privileges and Immunities of the United Nations." There is a long history of rebel forces scorning the authority of the U.N. and its documents. There remains today much more fear of the USA in the minds of rebel leaders than there is of the U.N. This fact alone means that a U.N. hostage is usually far worse off than a U.S. prisoner of war.

"This is a man without a country," Dave Sullivan explains, "covered by no law anywhere in the world. He loses the protection of the Geneva Convention. He is not subjected to the Uniform Code of Military Justice of the Armed Forces. He is in legal limbo."

Dave notes that the Administration admits there's a problem here, and has sought passage of yet another U.N. treaty, this one titled "The Convention on the Safety of United Nations and Associated Personnel." However, he said the U.S. hasn't even submitted it for Senate ratification. And even if it were to be ratified, it would amount to getting authorization from the U.N. for a self-evident U.S. right to protect our own soldiers. The proper solution is to simply stop the practice of forcing our troops to serve the U.N.

Captain Eugene "Red" McDaniel, AUS, (ret.)

Captain Eugene B. "Red" McDaniel has made a similar plea for our soldiers. One of the most prominent advocates of a full accounting of Americans missing in action or captured in foreign wars, Red was himself a Vietnam POW for more than six years, becoming one of the most brutally tortured at the hands of the Communist enemy in Hanoi. His position is forthright: "I'm very much opposed to putting U.S. troops under U.N. command. I think they should be under U.S. command at all times."

McDaniel notes cases of U.S. troops getting trapped in U.N. operations, including Marine Colonel Rich Higgins in Lebanon, and Army Chief Warrant Office Michael Durant in Somalia. Because of their U.N. status, Higgins was labeled a "hostage," not an American POW, when he was captured by terrorists. Durant was called a "detainee" when he was captured by the forces of Somali warlord Mohammad Farah Aidid. These designations mean that the U.S. military had no authority to rescue our own citizens, and that the American State Department was in charge of obtaining their freedom by talking about their plight and conducting "diplomacy."

Higgins was brutally killed and a videotape released by his terrorist kidnappers showed his lifeless body hanging from a rope. His dead body was later dumped on the streets of Beirut, Lebanon, on the birthday of his widow. Durant was eventually freed.

"My concern with the troops that are placed under U.N.

command is that if they become prisoners, they do not have the rights of the Geneva Convention," Red McDaniel says. Not only does this mean they can be denied basic standards of humanitarian treatment for POWs under the Geneva Convention, but their ambiguous legal status means there's bound to be some impact on their morale. "As a POW," McDaniel explains, "the only thing you have going for you is the belief that someday your country is going to come to get you. But had I not believed that when I was shot down, I could not have lived 6 years. I had to have absolute blind faith in my country. If I was asked to go again, would I go? Not before asking a lot of questions."

Sergeant First Class Ed Rasor, AUS, Special Forces

Sergeant Ed Rasor was particularly incensed to learn what was happening to Specialist Michael New. As a sergeant, he was appalled that Michael's sergeants weren't going to bat for him. "Where are his sergeants?!," he shouted. He discussed it among other Green Beret sergeants and found that he was not alone.

He made his points in a letter to Senator Jesse Helms, in the fall of 1995, informing the Senator that, as a combat medic with twelve years service, that he was not going to serve in a blue beret, that he had a Green Beret which he proudly wore. Furthermore, he stated that he would not deploy on any assignment with a foreign officer in command. And on top of that, he said that he would not agree to serve under the United Nations under any circumstances.

Even Ed was surprised when his fellow sergeants demanded that they be allowed to sign the letter too. So, in the end, ten senior non-commissioned officers signed that letter to the senator! All Special Forces. All top sergeants. All patriots. All risking their careers on behalf of their country.

Ed was told in 1996 that he would be receiving an honorable discharge from the U.S. Army based exclusively on his moral opposition to serving the United Nations. This means that other patriotic soldiers may be able to follow Rasor out of the military services without having their reputations damaged by a bad-conduct discharge, as with Michael New.

Finally, Sgt. Rasor put in a request for the promised honorable discharge. In his "personnel action" request, Ed had explained, "I base this request due to my firm belief that the involvement of members of the United States Armed Forces in United Nations military operations is unconstitutional."

After Sgt. Rasor spoke at a November, 1995, Washington news conference on behalf of Michael, he found himself on a "hit list" and was called into a meeting where he was told that the White House and Army headquarters were troubled by the exercise of his free speech rights against the U.N. That meant that his time was up, and he knew it.

In a dramatic development, Sgt. Rasor was told that he would have to resign from the Army. He was astounded. He told his Sergeant-Major, "I'm an enlisted man. Enlisted men cannot resign." The sergeant-major responded, "Sgt. Rasor, I thought the same thing until yesterday, when I was informed by visitors direct from the White House that the Commander in Chief will be pleased to accept your resignation."

First he resisted, then finally accepted. Then the Army changed their mind. It was a confusing and frustrating wait for Sgt. Rasor. He had previously withdrawn his application to Warrant Officer School, which had already been approved. He began thinking about whether he himself could order, or even advise, soldiers to serve the U.N,. and decided he could not do so. Yet his superiors were telling him that the U.S. military would be completely under U.N. control within the next 10 or 15 years.

It is tragic, of course, that the Army has lost such an outstanding soldier as Sgt. Rasor, along with most of the others who have refused to reenlist. A patriot who took his oath to defend the Constitution seriously, he had been speaking out against the Army's growing involvement in the U.N. for well over a year. His concern had been intensified by an article in *Special Warfare*, an official Army publication, which openly talked about the U.S. Army becoming a tool of "global reconstruction" in a world dominated by the U.N.[2] Rasor described the article as advocating that Special Forces be the "reconstruction tool for the New World Order."

Written by James J. Schneider, a professor of military theory at the School of Advanced Military Studies at the U.S. Army Command and General Staff College in Fort Leavenworth, Kansas, the article said the following:

"...[T]he future will be dominated by a resurgent force that will change the nature of both the nation-state and the national security system...

"We have yet to divine the full implications of the revolution in geopolitics euphemistically called the new world order.

"For the Army, and for Special Forces, the future will be a period of global reconstruction.

"But there is another aspect of reconstruction that anticipates the future — the Army's unique relationship to the U.S. Constitution.

"As an Army we are fortunate to have such a rich historical tradition. But this experience is of little use if it cannot be interpreted in light of future operations. In other words, to learn from the past we must anticipate the future. And the future will be dominated by a single overwhelming presence — the United Nations.

"One of the key legal strands was the right of the state to declare and wage war. The growing power of the U.N. is beginning slowly to erode this defining characteristic of the nation-state...

[2] Schneider, James J. "Ambushing the Future," Special Warfare. The Professional Bulletin of the John F. Kennedy Special Warfare Center and School, April 1995, pp. 2-10.

"Now, the U.N. has begun to redefine victory on its own terms.

"The U.N. redefinition of victory has also set the stage for redefining the purpose of a nation's armed forces... . The reemergence of the United Nations has created a new formula: Under the new U.N. arrangement of collective security, nations will strive primarily to compel peace.

"The U.N.'s central role in shaping the future during global reconstruction will persist, and its geopolitical influence will likely increase..."

[emphasis mine]

The reference in this article to the Army's "unique relationship" to the U.S. Constitution is strange indeed. An accurate reading of the Constitution and the soldier's oath would demonstrate that the Army's current role in the New World Order is incompatible with both. This is the critical fact that stared Ed Rasor in the face. At Fort Bragg, where Ed was based, he said there are many more soldiers "hungry for the truth" but consider the U.S. Constitution to be a controversial document that they would prefer to deal with as "underground literature." This reflects the pressure that is being brought to bear on soldiers to toe the pro-U.N. line.

The Army's delay in the case may have stemmed from a realization that the outcome could have had far-reaching implications — if it had been well-publicized. Allowing patriotic anti-U.N. soldiers to leave the service with an honorable discharge could have opened the door for more soldiers to follow Ed's example. Ed has said that many of his colleagues share his opposition to the U.N.

If enough soldiers take the route blazed by Ed Rasor, it might force President Clinton and top military officials to reevaluate their policy of integrating U.S. troops into U.N.

military operations.

So why did Army officials finally grant Rasor's request for an honorable discharge? It is likely that they figured it best to get rid of him, rather than risk having him remain and serve as an example from within that others might follow. They may also figure that his example will not be followed if the major media continue to refuse to cover the outcome of this extraordinary case.

In the meantime we are now getting word of other soldiers who have expressed a refusal to serve under the UN, and for the time being, are being given an Honorable Discharge.

The transformation of our military, however, has been captured in sporadic media reports such as the September 22, 1996 story that ran in the Staten Island (New York) Sunday Advance under the headline, "Army's new goal: Waging peace." In a story about Fort Bragg, where Ed was stationed, the reporter said that soldiers were "crammed into a classroom" studying "the art of negotiation" and how to "out-think and out-maneuver" an adversary. One of the techniques was using the silent stare to unnerve your opponent."[3]

Another such article appeared in the Washington Times under the headline, "General predicts high priority for U.S. peacekeeping." Bill Gertz reported that Pentagon leaders were discussing a "new defense strategy that would raise peacekeeping and humanitarian operations to high priorities...."

Reflecting this accelerating trend, the Army issued field manual 100-23, "Peace Operations," in December 1994. It declared,

"Peace operations have become increasingly common in the post-Cold War strategic security environment. For example, in its first 40 years, the United Nations (UN) conducted only 13 such operations, all relatively small, with the exception of UN operations in the

---

[3] David Wood, Newhouse News Service, "Army's new goal: Waging peace," *Staten Island Advance*, September 22, 1996.

Congo during the 1960s. Since 1988, the number of peace operations has more than doubled, with each succeeding one being more complex than the last."[4]

This field manual included excerpts from the U.N. charter, examples of U.N. resolutions and quotations from U.N. officials.

To facilitate Army involvement in U.N. operations, the U.S. Army Peacekeeping Institute was established at the U.S. Army War College at Carlisle Barracks, Pennsylvania. The Army even supplies aides to military advisers to the U.N. who are stationed at U.N. headquarters in New York City. One of them, Maj. Joseph F. Napoli, wrote an article for Army Times in which he declared, "Far from a perfect organization, the United Nations does not deserve the abuse it has received of late."[5]

This was a strange view to take. At the time, the director of U.N. military activities was Kofi Annan, who has since been elevated to the post of Secretary-General. Annan was a director and supervisor of the Somalia mission that resulted in 18 of Napoli's compatriots being slaughtered in the streets. An investigation conducted by Tom Farer, now the Dean of the Graduate School of International Studies at the University of Denver, identified Annan as one of the "main strategists and operational directors" at the U.N. of that failed "nation-building" scheme. Farer's remarks were included in a September 29, 1995, bipartisan U.S. Senate Report on the debacle prepared by Senators John Warner (R-Va.) and Carl Levin (D-Mich.).

Under Annan, the U.N. greatly expanded its military activities. Former Ambassador Frank Ruddy says Annan "never met an opportunity for multilateral assertiveness he didn't like." The *Earth Times*, a pro-U.N. publication, thought Annan's chances of becoming secretary-general were dead because he was "seen as wearing Bosnia as an albatross." In

---

[4] FM 100-23. Peace Operations, Headquarters, Department of the Army, December 1994, pp. iv-v.
[5] Joseph F. Napoli, "Current U.N.-bashing is way off base," *Army Times*, April 10, 1995.

Bosnia as well as Somalia, U.N. peacekeepers were forced to withdraw under humiliating circumstances. In Bosnia, of course, NATO then intervened.

Under Annan, the U.N.'s Office of Internal Oversight Services found that the U.N. "has lived without independent and effective oversight for decades" and that the peacekeeping area was plagued by waste. In a typical case, 59 containers of food rations were shipped to the U.N. military mission in Haiti, got spoiled in the hot sun and had to be destroyed at a cost of $40,000.

"The Army is the rapid reaction force for the Global Village."

Nevertheless, under Clinton's orders, the Army got more deeply involved in U.N. activities, issuing a 1996 "Army Vision 2010" document calling for more involvement in peacekeeping operations. At a news conference releasing the document, Army Chief of Staff Gen. Dennis J. Reimer said that "we've done the Somalias, the Bosnias, the Haitis, the security at the Olympics, and the firefighting in the Western states." He added, "The Army is the rapid reaction force for the global village."[6]

What's worse, our future military officers are being given a sympathetic treatment of foreign ideologies, including communism, at our military academies. Self-proclaimed Communist Pete Seeger was invited to give a 1997 lecture at West Point on "The Meaning of Freedom." Seeger had written a song celebrating North Vietnam Communist dictator Ho Chi Minh, and his songs were described by columnist Stephen Chapman as "a weapon in the service of a cause that has produced more suffering, destroyed more lives and piled up more corpses than any other form of government." Asked to explain Seeger's appearance, a West Point spokesman said it was important for cadets to give his views "respectful consideration." One wonders if West Point would like to provide their

---

[6] Patrick Pexton, "Future seizes operations other than war," *Army Times*, November 25, 1996, p. 8.

cadets with an opportunity to give the views of Spc. Michael New some 'respectful consideration'.

Not surprisingly, many soldiers can't take this. Many, in fact, are leaving the services. In addition to the objectionable nature of the globalist and even pro-Communist propaganda, so-called "peacekeeping" is a tremendous drain on the strength and morale of our soldiers. Colonel David Hackworth (Ret.), a decorated Vietnam veteran who is now a columnist, notes that many of the 37,000 who were sent by Clinton into the Persian Gulf, supposedly to threaten Saddam Hussein after he discontinued weapons inspections by the U.N., are burned out.

"Our warriors were rushed out there last February to do a job on Saddam Hussein," he notes. "They've been standing tall ever since. Besides being hot and sticky, they're bored to death, and sick of being cooped up. Their morale has plummeted from 'good to go' to 'wanna go home.' They feel like a fire department that was rushed to a fire only to find a false alarm, but then are told to 'hang around, a fire might start sometime this year.'"

"But should we expect anything else?" Hackworth asked. "This is the president who brought about the disaster in the streets of Mogadishu, and when 18 warriors died there, called them 'unfortunate casualties'; the same commander in chief who invaded Haiti to support a tyrant, whose gang of monsters has turned that poor island back into a killing field; and the same master of military miscalculation who sent our warriors to Bosnia in 1995 for one year — and three years later they're still marking time on Mission Impossible."[7]

The Resister

Nevertheless, some soldiers have chosen to remain in the military and express their dissent in other ways. A publication called *The Resister*, which openly opposes U.S. military involvement with the U.N., has emerged as an outlet for many

---

[7] Colonel David Hackworth, (Ret.), "Bring the Fire Department Home, *Soldier of Fortune*, August 1998, p. 82.

of these soldiers, who secretly write for it under various pseudonyms.

In an editorial entitled, "In Defense of Specialist Michael New," the editors said:

"The Oath of Enlistment is a sworn allegiance to the legal and philosophical foundations of this nation represented by the Constitution and the writings of the Framers... . Adherence to contrary philosophies, support of contradictory political systems, or advocacy of institutions and organizations that undermine the Constitution is, at best, subversion. Actively working to advance contrary philosophies, promote contradictory political systems, and participation in institutions and organizations that undermine the Constitution is nothing less than treason...

"The U.N. is a foreign power by definition, and it is a foreign enemy by its actions. In the United States, persons who promote the U.N. and organizations that advance it are domestic enemies and traitors.

"Keeping the above in mind, any United States soldier who voluntarily promotes the U.N. and willingly serves under U.N. command in any capacity is violating the oath he took to support and defend the Constitution against all enemies, foreign and domestic.' Any United States soldier who serves under U.N. auspices is serving a foreign power under foreign command and therefore abrogates his status as a United States soldier. His loyalty has been transferred and his oath has been negated....

"Specialist Michael New...has demonstrated the moral integrity and principled action of a truly honorable man...

"Specialist New's chain of command is not concerned with issues of moral integrity, honor or the unconstitutionality of transferring a U.S. soldier's loyalty to a hostile foreign power against his will…

"The hypocrisy of SPC New's chain of command, and the injustice of the issue involved here, is that officers have the option of resigning their commission in protest to orders they believe to be illegal or unconstitutional. Enlisted soldiers cannot resign. They either obey and compromise their moral integrity, or they disobey and are punished."[8]

The Resister, however, took a different approach than Michael. Some soldiers associated with this magazine, which once advertised itself as "The Official Publication of the Special Forces Underground," did not refuse orders to serve on U.N.-controlled missions. Rather, they decided to go on these missions and undermine them from within. One member of the group told The American Legion Magazine, "No member of the Special Forces Underground is going to refuse an order to go anywhere or do anything. But what is going to happen is that, in any U.N.-directed show, we'll do everything in our power to subvert those goals." He added, "Our approach is simply different than that of Michael New. We know it's a violation of our oath, so we're just going to make sure the mission doesn't succeed."[9]

Strong words, clearly demonstrating the depth of the anti-U.N sentiment that currently exists in the Armed Forces, and particularly in the Special Forces. Special Forces troops don't get where they are by blindly putting their brains in neutral and doing the day-to-day tasks. When you select men for their ability to think, you then have to contend with the problem that they retain their ability to think. In a totalitarian State, this is a major problem. In a free country with citizen-soldiers, this is a major source of strength, even with the problems inherent in soldiers who actually think. It's both a weakness and a

[8] "In Defense of Specialist Michael New, *The Resister*, Vol. II, No. 2
[9] Cliff Kincaid, "Oath of Uncertainty," *The American Legion Magazine*, July 1996, p.50.

strength.

U.S. forces in Haiti said to be associated with The Resister were linked in the press to opposition political activities there.[10] The regime of Marxist President Jean-Bertrand Aristide had asked for the U.N. or the U.S. to investigate these allegations. There is no question that coming under U.N. command in Haiti and restoring Aristide to power was a bitter pill to swallow for many of our Special Forces soldiers. One wrote to Soldier of Fortune magazine saying he was disgusted by what was happening:

> "Not only did we fall under U.N. command, but we were made to trade in our green berets for blue. That's right, we were stripped of the presidential award that distinguishes us from the rest and made to wear head gear that robs everyone of their identity.

> "Yesterday we were ordered to take down our Stars and Stripes because we did not have a U.N. flag to fly with it...We feel as if we have been sold out by our own command."[11]

Something similar happened in Bosnia, where the Los Angeles Times reported that the American flag was banned. The truth was not quite so dramatic. It turned out that the Stars and Stripes continued to be flown over each American base camp but was banned from vehicle antennas and tents. A Pentagon official explained that the red, white and blue would detract from the "multinational" character of the mission.

While actions by soldiers associated with The Resister in these "multinational" missions were controversial, the publication itself found it was striking a chord. Some soldiers who were found with copies of it were reprimanded. Yet, in an article in the Colorado Springs Gazette Telegraph, reporter Genevieve Anton noted that the Army had no basis on which to suppress the publication because it does not advocate racism, illegal actions or violence. In fact, the reporter said, a

[10] Douglas Farah and Dana Priest, "Haiti Says U.S. Troops May have Helped Foes," The Washington Post, December 8, 1995, p. 43.

[11] "SF Under U.N. Command," Letter to the Editor, Soldier of Fortune, September 1995, p.80

review of several issues found "mostly intellectual discussions" of various issues.

The existence of *The Resister* stands as evidence of the serious impact the Michael New controversy has had on the Armed Forces.

The blunt truth is that our civilian and military leaders are putting our soldiers into an untenable position. After having enticed them into serving the U.S. military under the terms of a sacred oath to the Constitution, those leaders are then ordering them to change their allegiance. If these leaders were being honest about it, they would openly call for changing the oath to accommodate the interests of the U.N. But, of course, they won't do that.

LTC Guy Cunningham – 29 Palms Survey

These leaders won't come forward and advocate changing the oath because they understand that most of our troops would not swear an oath to the U.N. A survey of soldiers conducted by Lieutenant Commander Ernest G. "Guy" Cunningham (USN) revealed that more than 60 percent would never take an oath of allegiance to the U.N. Cunningham's thesis, "Peacekeeping and U.N. Operational Control: A Study of Their Effect on Unit Cohesion," was based on a survey of 300 Marines on May 10, 1994. It was perhaps the first, and remains the best systematic analysis of whether our troops themselves believe involvement with the U.N. compromises their oaths as American soldiers. Asked if they agreed or disagreed with the statement that, "I feel there is no conflict between my oath of office and serving as a U.N. soldier," fifty-seven percent disagreed. They were also asked if they would swear to a U.N. code similar to their own military oath. The code said, "I am a United Nations fighting person. I serve in the forces which maintain world peace and every nation's way of life I am prepared to give my life in their defense." Sixty-nine percent said they would refuse.

There was some controversy at the time about whether Cunningham's thesis was somehow designed to further the U.N. agenda. Among certain groups that controversy lingers today. Much attention was focused on one question in particular Question 46 – whether U.S. troops on a U.N. mission would open fire on American citizens "who refuse or resist confiscation of firearms banned by the U.S. Government." Anti-gun control groups were outraged that the question was even asked. But the answer was very informative. It found that 26 percent were prepared to carry out such a mission. Fortunately, most said they would not.

As James Pate reported in Soldier of Fortune magazine, "...several publications unfairly vilified Cunningham as some sort of New World Order fiend." But Pate, among others, met extensively with Guy, and found him to be a committed patriot. Indeed, he comes from a family with an impressive military background, having served in the military with his father and two of his brothers. A staunch anti-communist, he wanted to serve in Vietnam but was assigned to the 101st Airborne when that unit was being withdrawn from the conflict. He received Army medical training, joined Special Forces in 1977, went into the active reserves, and then resigned and went into the Navy, where he became a pilot and flight instructor.

Rather than being part of an effort to soften up our troops for U.N. duty, Guy Cunningham was blowing the whistle from within. Guy was an insider who was able to study this issue from a unique vantage point. "I realized my opportunity to do something that basically no one else could," he said. "I was in the right place at the right time. My mission was to bring to a higher awareness, from a different perspective, the potential loss of the American soldiers identity that would result from the administration's pro-U.N. policy."

In an article about Michael's case, Guy went after those further up in the chain of command, noting:

> "If the response of the chain of command down to
> New was a statement along the lines of the signifi-
> cance of this [U.N.] mandate never occurred to us,
> then this suggests ineptitude. If the response by the
> chain of command acknowledges their understanding
> of this order, then this order represents another step
> toward the progressive pogrom of the American
> fighting man's identity."[12]

A variation of this problem occurs when the U.N. gets
involved in a conflict or country in which American soldiers
have been involved. In 1991, when the American military was
assisting a democratically-elected government in El Salvador,
two of our soldiers, Lt. Colonel David Pickett and Cpl. Ernest
Dawson, were shot down, taken prisoner and murdered by
Communist terrorists. Their killers were apprehended and
jailed. But El Salvador's Supreme Court then ruled that a
U.N.-brokered peace agreement had necessitated their release.
Pickett's father, retired Colonel Edward F. Pickett, sought justice from the U.N. as well as the State Department. Both
claimed their hands were tied because El Salvador was a sovereign nation.

So justice was once again denied, with the confused lines of
authority and control set up by the United Nations. In this
game, the U.N. hides behind the authority of a sovereign
nation, while the sovereign nation hides behind the authority
of treaties with the United Nations.

This is similar to the game Department of the Army lawyers
have played, arguing in civilian courts that Michael New cannot be tried there because this is a military matter – "lack of
jurisdiction." At the same time, when facing a military tribunal, they have argued that because there are political implications in this case, it is "non-justiciable," or out of the jurisdiction of the military courts. In effect, Bill Clinton has rendered

---

[12] Guy Cunningham, "Green Team or Blue Team. Specialist New: A Prisoner of Conscience?",   8,
February 1996, p. 32.

all armed forces serving under the U.N. without a "swift and imperative legal remedy," which virtually leaves Michael New "a man without a country." Certainly he has, to date, been a man without Constitutional protection.

Chief Petty Officer Duane Thorin, USN, (ret.)

A generation ago, Duane Thorin, Navy helicopter pilot and former POW in Korea, spoke out forcefully on this issue. I am grateful to Mr. Thorin for his permission to use the following notes, which I have edited, from an unpublished manuscript.

In testimony before a U.S. Senate subcommittee, Thorin posed this question to Senator Symington, of Missouri:[13]

"When it is proposed that all nations shall provide military forces to the United Nations organization, it should be made clear, and this is simple enough to say, whether or not American soldiers would then owe prior allegiance to the dictates of the Secretary-General, or of the Security Council of the United Nations, or whether they still would hold their prior allegiance to the Constitution of the United States."

Symington replied,

"I am not sure I fully understood what the United States just presented to the world in its disarmament offer. But it is my understanding that the ultimate goal was a world army that would control all countries. Is that correct?"

Thorin responded,

"Well, sir, I cannot say whether or not that is correct. I will say this is also my understanding. And frankly, Senator, I don't want our country controlled by any army. Do you?"

The Senator did not answer the witness' question, but was visibly shaken by it (and the question was deleted from the published record of the hearings). After a few inane remarks

[13] April, 1962, hearings of the Special Preparedness Subcommittee of the Senate Committee of Armed Services.

and rhetorical questions, Symington departed the hearing room. His simple, yet accurate categorization of the ultimate goal of the disarmament proposal issued by the U.S. State Department in September, 1961, had been a hurried comment to evade a more direct response to this previous question posed by the witness:

> No promoter or advocate of that 1961 "disarmament" proposal is known to have publicly answered or even entertained that question regarding a soldier's allegiance. Rather, whenever American servicemen have been ordered into the service of the United Nations, the appeal has been to patriotism and/or national pride.

"But the answer is now vividly apparent in the recent court-martial of U.S. Army Specialist Michael New. His refusal to wear the uniform and insignia of the United Nations has resulted for him in a Bad Conduct Discharge. That was handed down from "higher authorities" via Lt. Col. Gary Jewell, who headed the military tribunal without opportunity for Soldier New or his attorneys to present to the panel of officers and enlisted men any evidence or testimonies in defense of his actions.

"Clearly, then, domestic promoters and minions of the 'New World Order', expressly including the current commander-in-chief of our Armed Forces, and at least some of the upper echelons thereof – regard an oath to support and defend the U.S. Constitution to be insignificant, a mere formality, perhaps. Or, it may in some cases indicate such ignorance of certain principles of the Constitution that they don't realize what an oath thereunto commits one to support and defend.

"In any case, they obviously regard a soldier with a sense of dedication to his country's Constitution, and the courage to openly express it to now be unsuited for service in our nation's Armed Forces. There is some logic here, since it is their intent that he ultimately shall serve some supranational authority[14] based on political principles directly contrary to those of our Constitution, and to which it is intended that our nation will be subordinated along with all others.

"Service in a 'world army' committed to control of all countries would not require loyalty to any political or moral principles, but rather forbids it. It requires instead the rationale of a mercenary soldier – mindless subservience and obedience to orders from whomever is in command. This is similar to that level of obedience expected of the Nazi guards at Auschwitz who pled at their trials in Nuremberg that they were only 'following orders' when they forced innocent people into the gas chambers."

Thorin has capably pointed out that much of the work for planning the end of our sovereignty had already been worked out at the famous Pugwash Conferences between 1955 and 1965.[15]

Duane Thorin has captured the essence of the problem by referring to U.S. troops as having being transformed from "Defenders of Liberty" to "Keepers of Peace," to "Enforcers of Peace." The U.N. role in these conflicts compromises the ability of our fighting personnel to defend American interests and to be defended by America when they put their lives on the line.

In the eyes of Mr. Clinton and his State Department, the time for national sovereignty has come to an end, and the time for the New World Order has dawned. Nationalism has become the new enemy of civilization.

No one would accuse Arthur Schlesinger, Jr., of being a member of some shadowy "right wing conspiracy." A long

[14] It needs to be noted that while the UN is prescribed to be the controlling agency in the State Department's 1961 disarmament proposal, it is not essential to continuance toward transformation of our armed forces into part of that "world army" to control all countries. Only some manner of supranational controlling agency would be required, no matter its name. The Bosnia commitment as a NATO operation exemplifies such an alternative. There are indications that President Clinton originally intended for that deployment to be under UN control, but switched to NATO because of publicity arising from SPC New's refusal to serve as a UN soldier in Macedonia.

[15] Thorin, Duane, The Pugwash Movement and U.S. Army Policy, subtitled "Should Weapons Systems be placed under 'International Control'?," Monte Cristo Press, New York, 1965.

time left-wing voice for global government, he recently wrote in *Foreign Affairs*:

"Can we want [the United Nations] to dwindle into impotence, leaving the world to the anarchy of nation states? We are not going to achieve a new world order without paying for it in blood as well as in words and money."[16]

Schlesinger is not writing about his own blood. He's referring to the blood of my children and yours. I have said on radio and in speaking engagements across this nation, "The blood of my children and grandchildren is not available to be sacrificed on the altar of the New World Order!" Time will tell how many Americans agree.

According to former U.S. Ambassador Jeane Kirkpatrick, "We are slipping into practices which enhance only the power of the strongest. Is this what we want to do? Someone had better think through this question — and soon."[17]

[16] Schlesinger, "Back to the Womb?" article in Foreign Affairs, July/August, 1995.
[17] Jeane Kirkpatrick. "When Should the Tanks Roll?" The Washington Post. 17 October 1994:A-19.

Chapter 4

MERCENARY ARMY
★ ★ ★ ★

"Dying for world order when there is no concrete threat to one's own nation is a hard argument to make. For understandable reasons, our leaders are not making it. We have a professional army made up of men and women who volunteered for the job, and the job, alas, may include fighting, killing and dying. But let a few American soldiers get killed and the congressional and popular demand for withdrawal becomes almost irresistible."
—Arthur Schlesinger, Jr., Foreign Affairs,
July-August 1995, pp. 7-8

Since Michael took his stand in favor of American sovereignty and against U.N. control of our troops, much has happened, and the situation has dramatically deteriorated. In a sense, the problem that he focused attention on – U.N. command and control of U.S. troops in Macedonia in the former Yugoslavia – has become somewhat minor. After all, only a few thousand U.S. troops have been deployed to Macedonia wearing the U.N. uniform, and always around 500 at a time.

Today, however, tens of thousands of U.S. troops are serving the U.N. but without wearing the U.N. uniform. A March 1997 Pentagon document stated that **68,790** U.S. troops were involved in U.N.-authorized or international peacekeeping activities. This figure included U.S. "blue-helmeted" personnel in Macedonia (said to be 511) as well as 1,052 personnel involved in "non-UN Peace Operations" in the Middle East and Latin America It also included 67,200 troops "supporting enforcement" of U.N. Security Council resolutions in Bosnia, Iraq, and Korea. In other words, according to the Pentagon itself, there were approximately 68,000 "green-helmeted"

U.S. troops serving the U.N.

The UN's World Army has, therefore, arrived, and American soldiers are the front line troops.

This was dramatically demonstrated when U.N. Secretary-General **Kofi Annan**, after returning from Baghdad, Iraq, with a "deal" to allow limited inspections of Saddam Hussein's weapons sites, made the astounding statement that, "Together we are the ultimate power." This was an endorsement of the U.N. becoming a world government, in which the once-great United States plays the role of bit player, (and financier) while our interests are subservient to whatever power running the United Nations.

If policy makers ever needed any additional evidence that the U.N. was out-of-control, this statement about "the ultimate power" was it.

In another extraordinary statement, Annan said that U.S. and British military power in the Gulf region had contributed to Iraq's acceptance of the deal, and that President Clinton and British Prime Minister Tony Blair had performed as "perfect U.N. peacekeepers." This was a reference to their deployment of some 37,000 troops U.S. and British troops to the Gulf. Thus, Annan was labeling Clinton and Blair as mere pawns of the world body. While Mr. Clinton may have seen this as a compliment, there are others throughout American history who could have only regarded it as treasonous to give away American sovereignty or to entangle us in foreign alliances from which we cannot be easily extracted.

No amount of rhetoric about the U.S. being "the last remaining superpower" can obscure the fact that it is clearly the United Nations which is on the road to becoming the real superpower, with U.S. troops operating as a rapid deployment force for the world body. This is the official Clinton policy.

This has been the policy of every administration, in fact, of both parties at least since President Kennedy, who outlined in State Department Document 7277 in 1961 that the American government is working toward the day when the United Nations will have a large standing army capable of preventing any nation from waging war, while national armies are to be reduced to national police forces. Furthermore, it is currently being proposed by powerful voices in the United Nations that in order to achieve this global vision of John Kennedy's State Department, that all military bases of every nation will have to be turned over the control of the United Nations.[1]

Vice President Gore supports this trend, having told parents of U.S. troops who died in a "friendly fire" incident over Iraq that they "could be proud that they had died in service to the U.N." As parents, we don't think most Americans would be proud of that assertion.

Increasingly, Americans are being deployed on behalf of interests that have no relationship at all to protecting American interests. In 1997, U.S. Army deployments around the globe reached the 100-country mark for the first time in history. "The increasing number of deployments reflects a willingness by the Clinton Administration to use the military for a variety of humanitarian and peacekeeping missions in the aftermath of the Cold War. The Army and the other services also are busier now with multinational exercises, particularly in Europe and the Asia-Pacific region," one report said.[2]

By July 1998, the Washington Post reported that American special operations forces had "established military ties in at least 110 countries."[3] It said these involve many U.N.-style "training exercises" with countries such as former Communist or Soviet- aligned countries as Kazakhstan, Madagascar, Mongolia, Russia and Uzbekistan. "Plans are in the works for the first such exercises involving U.S. and Chinese troops

[1] Fisas, Vicen, BLUE GEOPOLITICS, The United Nations Reform and the Future of the Blue Helmets. Foreword by UNESCO Director-General Federico Mayor Zaragoza, Pluto Press, London, 1995. 184 pages

[2] "U.S. Soldiers deployed in 100 countries," The Baltimore Sun, May 24, 1997, p.5.

[3] Dana Priest, "Sidestepping Sanctions, U.S. Military Trains Foreign Troops," The Washington Post, July 12, 1998, p.1.

next year," the paper said. In Africa, the Post reported that U.S. forces had trained the militaries of 31 out of 54 African countries. Six of these countries – Ghana, Malawi, Senegal, Uganda, Mali, and Ethiopia – were receiving training to participate in a state Department-led African Crisis Response Initiative, a regional peacekeeping force.

In July 1998, the U.S. Air National Guard hosted a training exercise involving European forces that went under the bizarre title, "Global Patriot." More than 15,000 service members from the Air National Guard, Air Force, Air Force Reserve, U.S. Army, Army Reserve, Navy and Marines were joined by Dutch, British, Paraguayan and Canadian forces.

In Europe, according to the Pentagon's own figures, the U.S. troops deployed on the NATO mission in Bosnia are there on behalf of the U.N. This helps demonstrate the link between NATO and the U.N.

The groundwork for intervention in Bosnia, formerly part of Communist Yugoslavia, was laid by George Soros, who emigrated to the U.S. from Hungary and became a billionaire through financial speculation in the world's currency markets. His foundation has put millions of dollars into various projects in the former Communist countries in Europe, including Bosnia. He is a big backer of the U.N. and has said that as long as the U.N. cannot fulfill its military mission, NATO should move ahead because it "has the potential of serving as the basis for a new world order" in Europe. Bosnia is a test for his theory.

Soros established the "Committee for American Leadership in Bosnia," which took out advertisements in various newspapers urging American intervention. The ads made much of the fact, as Clinton did, that the mission in Bosnia would supposedly "be a NATO operation, with clear lines of command, under an American general." This seemed to be an important concession to the strong objections that had been voiced to

Clinton's previous practice of putting our troops at the disposal of the United Nations. It was also a response to the disastrous record of the U.N. peacekeeping troops in Bosnia.

It is technically true that the Bosnia deployment is not "led" by the U.N. in the sense that our troops are commanded and controlled by the world body. Our soldiers aren't wearing the U.N. uniform consisting of U.N. patches, insignia and berets. But even the Pentagon concedes it is a U.N. "authorized" operation. In the long run, this may be more effective than outright U.N. control.

The key passage in the "peace agreement," the so-called Dayton accord that was hammered out between the warring factions, was Article VI, describing the circumstances under which the "Implementation Force" (IFOR), composed of troops from NATO and non-NATO nations, would be deployed. The U.N. Security Council, composed of the U.S., Russia, China, France and England, was "invited to authorize Member States or regional organizations and arrangements to establish the IFOR acting under Chapter VII of the United Nations Charter." This may sound innocuous, but the officials at the Clinton State Department who put this together knew exactly what they were doing. It meant, essentially, that the IFOR became a U.N. operation. This is so because Chapter VII of the U.N. Charter gives the Security Council the blanket authority to "maintain or restore international peace and security." In a different section of the U.N. Charter, Chapter VIII, Articles 52-54 enable the world body to authorize the use of "regional arrangements or agencies" for the "maintenance of international peace and security." This is the role that NATO is fulfilling in Bosnia.

The U.N.'s fingerprints on the operation were found on the very first page of the peace agreement, whereby the parties agreed to "conduct their relations in accordance with the principles set forth in the United Nations charter."

Other provisions filled in the details of what Clinton was talking about when he told the American people that there was a role for the "international community" and "civilian agencies" in reconstructing Bosnia. These included the appointment of a "High Representative," backed by the U.N., with broad authority over all civilian matters. An office of human rights "ombudsman" was to be established and the parties were required to "join in inviting" the United Nations Commission on Human Rights and "other intergovernmental or regional human rights" missions into the area. They were also supposed to provide "full and unrestricted access" by such organizations as the U.N. Development Program.

Nowhere was the U.N.'s role more obvious than Annex 11 of the agreement, concerning establishment of an "International Police Task Force." This was explicitly defined as a U.N.-established operation whose Commissioner will be appointed by the U.N. Secretary-General. Its role includes monitoring and inspecting law enforcement and judicial activities, training law enforcement personnel, and making sure free and fair elections in Bosnia are carried out. In essence, the U.N. was creating a police force in Bosnia.

The history is important. In Somalia, the U.N. tried to disarm the factions and register their weapons. In Haiti, the U.N. and the U.S. threw out one regime and replaced it with another. In Bosnia, the U.N. and NATO are trying to build a democratic state from scratch.

The U.S. State Department even wrote the country's constitution, which is part of the peace agreement. It says it is "Guided by the Purposes and Principles of the Charter of the United Nations" and is "inspired" by several U.N. treaties on human rights. Moreover, in Annex I, the Bosnian government is told that it has to enforce a series of international agreements, including the 1989 U.N. Convention on the Rights of the Child, which hasn't even been ratified here in the U.S.

The fact that individuals indicted as war criminals by the U.N-sponsored International Tribunal for the former Yugoslavia were prohibited from holding political office in Bosnia was portrayed in an extremely positive light. U.S. forces have been deployed to round up these suspects. But those concerned about legality were troubled by the fact that there is no authority for the U.N. to run such a judicial proceeding. The tribunals (there is another concerning Rwanda) are supposed to be based on Chapter VII of the U.N. Charter, but this authorizes U.N. military operations, not the creation of criminal courts. The creation of these tribunals represents a blatant power grab by the U.N. designed to lay the groundwork for an International Criminal Court.

But NATO's link to the U.N. goes far back – to the North Atlantic Treaty itself. The document which established NATO declares that "The Parties to this Treaty reaffirm their faith in the purposes and principles of the Charter of the United Nations..."

Before NATO formally expanded to include three more countries, a charter was signed between NATO and Russia which makes it clear that NATO has become a military arm of the U.N. and that Russian and American troops will work together in the future to police the world. The agreement refers explicitly to NATO having "...taken on new missions of peacekeeping and crisis management in support of the United Nations (UN) and the Organization for Security and Cooperation in Europe (OSCE), such as in Bosnia and Herzegovina."

Thus, the Bosnia deployment is confirmed to be a U.N. operation and model for future military activities. And just what is the OSCE? It is a European security organization that includes the U.S., Russia, and many former Soviet-bloc countries. It is currently working with the U.N. in Bosnia.

What Clinton has done, with the support of a Republican

Senate, is bring about creation of a U.N. Army through NATO, a process that has been largely non-controversial because of the general public perception that NATO served a worthwhile purpose as a defensive alliance against Soviet aggression. Clinton and his backers realized that NATO had a much better reputation than the U.N. Most Republicans, with such notable exceptions as Senator John Ashcroft (R-Mo.), were reluctant to challenge him.

We've been told by more than one congressmen that the controversy over the case of Army Specialist Michael New may have been a factor in convincing Clinton and his top aides that massive induction of American soldiers into a blue-helmeted U.N. Army was not possible. So, rather than make all of these troops wear U.N. uniforms, including blue berets and U.N. shoulder patches, they are being deployed under the auspices of NATO, wearing their green Army uniforms. It's a massive deception.

The use of NATO as a military arm of the U.N. has almost as many legal and constitutional problems as the deployment to Macedonia.

When NATO engaged in massive air strikes on Serbian positions during the Bosnian civil war, it became an active participant in that war. NATO became part of the Implementation Force (IFOR) and later the Stabilization Force (SFOR) in the former Yugoslavia. And it was all done illegally.

As noted by former foreign service officer Harold Eberle, "The North Atlantic Treaty, by intent, explicit verbiage, and its legislative history, created a wholly defensive alliance. Article 5, which is the core of the Pact, states that the parties agree that an armed attack against one or more of them in Europe or North America will be considered as an attack against all of them, and all will in concert with one another 'take such action as necessary, including the use of armed force' to restore and maintain the security of the North Atlantic area (defined in the

Treaty as the signatory powers and their islands north of the Tropic of Cancer). Article 11 says that the Treaty shall be ratified and carried out by the parties "in accordance with their respective constitutional processes."

"Had any of the belligerents in Bosnia committed armed aggression against any NATO signatory nation? Quite the opposite. The U.S. attacked them."

Eberle points out that Senator Arthur Vandenberg (R-Mich.), the pivotal figure during the Foreign Relations Committee's 16-day NATO hearings in April 1949, queried Secretary of State Dean Acheson about the precise limits of the Treaty: "It is not my understanding that it would come into effect on the basis of contemplation; the armed attack has to occur. Am I wrong on that?" Acheson: "You are right, Senator."

Vandenberg pressed on: "...no nation is the target of this Treaty unless it nominates itself as an armed aggressor. Is that right?" Acheson: "Yes, sir; that is correct."

Eberle comments, "There is no doubt that the Vandenberg-Acheson colloquy on Articles 5 and 11 was responsible for the Treaty unanimously clearing the Committee 13-0, and being ratified 82-13 by an otherwise reluctant full Senate. Had ex-law professor William J. Clinton's current tortured justification for its application today in Bosnia been expounded back in 1949, the Treaty would never have been favorably reported by the Foreign Relations Committee nor adopted by the Senate."

Indeed, the whole point of the Vandenberg-Acheson exchange was precisely to assure the Congress and the nation (as well as Europe and Soviet leaders) that no future President could possibly distort the intent of the Treaty. The very words "take such action as necessary" and "in accordance with their constitutional processes" were deliberately inserted into the Treaty by Vandenberg to preserve the Congress's war declaration powers.

Yet President Clinton, without prior Congressional approval, ordered American troops into Bosnia under the aegis of NATO, along with military contingents from dozens of other nations. Eberle commented that the president was converting a limited defensive alliance "into a multinational Boy Scout pack with a series of rhetorical flip-flops to justify his ill-conceived commitment, the consequences of which no one can accurately predict, and for which no vital American interest exists other than proving American leadership."

Actually, the American "interest" seems to lie in working with the U.N. to create an Islamic state in the heart of Europe. The Bosnian Muslims, whom we are supporting, also receive assistance from the Arab/ Muslim bloc, including Saudi Arabia and Iran. Bosnian President Alija Izetbegovic is said to have made the following declaration in his book, Muslim Declaration:

> "There can be no peace or coexistence between Islamic faith and non-Islamic faith and institutions...The Islamic movement must and can take power as soon as it is morally and numerically strong enough, not only to destroy the non-Islamic power, but to build up a new Islamic one..."

Why have American military personnel been put in the position of fighting and dying on behalf of a Muslim state in Europe?

As this book was going to press, it appeared America was preparing to go to war under the aegis of NATO in a place called Kosovo, also on behalf of Muslims. By and large, the media had treated the issue as something that required no significant national debate. On ABC's This Week with Sam Donaldson and Cokie Roberts on June 14, Senate Majority Leader Trent Lott was asked a grand total of two questions about NATO's pending decision to intervene, to risk American lives in the conflict. Lott's answers, which were in favor of intervention, were indistinguishable from the policy of the Clinton Administration.

Panelist George Will asked a simple question: What's the American interest there and how important is it? Lott never answered the question. Instead, he said it had global implications and that America ought to be prepared to act. Asked whether American troops ought to be used, Lott talked about the seriousness of the situation and said that we can't wait forever.

These pitiful answers to serious questions were largely ignored because George Will had prefaced the question by saying that ethnic cleansing was taking place in Kosovo. That is guaranteed to get a politician to endorse some kind of action for any reason. Politicians don't want to appear soft on human rights violations. But the human rights violations in this case are taking place on both sides. If the Yugoslavian government is guilty of ethnic cleansing, the Kosovo Liberation Army has been guilty of waging terrorist attacks. Senator Lott and the Administration both wanted the U.S. to get involved right in the middle of this.

On what basis? How does the U.S. or NATO justify intervening in a conflict in a foreign country? The so-called "international community" agreed that Kosovo, where the violence was taking place, is a part of Yugoslavia. Therefore, it should be an internal matter. On that level it's comparable to America's civil war. Even if we were dealing with two separate countries, how does NATO justify a decision to intervene? As Harold Eberle points out, the NATO charter, article 5, says NATO is obligated to come to the defense of its member states. NATO recently admitted three new members, Poland, Hungary and the Czech Republic, but Kosovo isn't one of them.

It's true that the recent Senate vote on NATO expansion included a reference to "other missions" for NATO. It said that NATO can engage in these "other missions" when there is a consensus among its members "that there is a threat to the security and interests of NATO members." Is this vague formulation the basis for NATO's actions on Kosovo? If so, then NATO can intervene anywhere in the world for almost any reason. If this is the case, when and why should the Congress retain its constitutional right to declare war and make the rules and regulations for the Armed Forces?

It's becoming apparent that Congress is being (voluntarily) cut out of the process, and that NATO is acting as a crucial element of an emerging U.N. army. These are the "other missions" it is undertaking. Sending our troops directly to Kosovo would be explained in terms of stopping more bloodshed, but the deployment could also turn out to resemble the one in Bosnia – with no end in sight. NATO expansion means more such endless commitments in the future.

Tragically, no-win wars have become rather common to Americans. Since World War II, in fact, the United States has not won a war in the sense of total military victory, the destruction of an enemy, and the occupation of enemy territory. The Korean War, fought under U.N. auspices, was a deliberate stalemate, the Vietnam War was lost by politicians who prohibited victory, and the Persian Gulf War was terminated before total victory was achieved.

In Korea, the critical point came in 1951, when U.N. forces were on the offensive and General Douglas MacArthur was calling for total victory, including air and ground attacks on the Chinese Mainland. MacArthur was then relieved of his command by President Truman and cease-fire discussions began in response to a proposal by the Soviet Union for U.N.-sponsored truce talks. In Korea, retired Major General John K. Singlaub noted that America "accepted a strange new concept: limited war." Today, we still have 37,000 U.S. troops in South Korea that are under U.N. control.

Virtually the same thing happened in the Gulf War. General Norman Schwarzkopf, the commander of the Gulf War effort, has explained that the war was terminated because U.N. resolutions which authorized the war effort allowed our forces to evict the Iraqi Army from Kuwait, but not to pursue the enemy to its capital and military headquarters in Baghdad.

The concept of "limited war" also applied in the Vietnam conflict, started by North Vietnamese Communist Ho Chi Minh, using a phony "indigenous" movement in the South called the Viet Cong. Curiously, General Schwarzkopf has written that one of the reasons the U.S. lost in Vietnam was a failure to obtain "international legitimacy," such as the U.N., for our intervention. He ignores the fact that the U.N. was then undergoing a dramatic transformation from the time when it was considered an organization dominated by the U.S. to one dominated by the Soviets and their client states. U.N. backing for the Vietnam War would have been foolish and unsuccessful. And the fact is, the entire Vietnam fiasco was fought under the auspices of SEATO, which was a "regional arrangement" identical to NATO. History shows clearly that the U.S. lost the war because there was a failure of political will and because an objective of total victory was never pursued. What is not so clear is that many of our actions were constantly thwarted or compromised by forces within SEATO who were favorable to the Communists.[4]

During the Reagan and Bush Administrations, things changed. Some military actions were undertaken that had decisive outcomes. These included the invasion and liberation of Grenada and Panama. It is noteworthy that U.N. approval of these operations was not sought. Indeed, if such approval had been sought, it would not have been given. Russia (then

---

[4] SEPTEMBER 8, 1954. The Southeast Asia Collective Defense Treaty was signed by the eight participating nations, including the United States. The Southeast Asia Treaty Organization (SEATO), as a regional subsidiary of the UN, later served as the primary "legal" justification for U.S. involvement in Vietnam. Writing in the New York Times for March 2, 1966, C. L. Sulzberger revealed that former Secretary of State John Foster Dulles "fathered SEATO with the deliberate purpose, as he explained to me, of providing the U.S. President with legal authority to intervene in Indochina." After the war, which formally ended with a communist victory on April 30, 1975, SEATO, having served its purpose, was disbanded (February 1976). Source: The New American, April 3, 1995, UNITED NATIONS CHRONOLOGY: FIFTY YEARS OF SHAME, by Robert W. Lee.

the Soviet Union), China and perhaps France would have used their vetoes on the Security Council to prohibit U.N. endorsement of such military operations.

Reagan's major successes in foreign policy, including the liberation of Grenada and support for anti-communist movements in Nicaragua and Afghanistan, had to be implemented completely outside of U.N. channels. If Reagan had depended on the U.N. to further American interests, we would probably be facing a Communist Central America and an expanding Soviet empire today.

Under Bill Clinton there has been a dramatic acceleration of a long-standing trend. American foreign and military policy has been conducted consistently in deference to the U.N. In fact, Clinton has endeavored to get the U.S. more deeply involved in a wide variety of U.N. operations. Somalia remains the most obvious example. It's true that President Bush had first deployed our troops to Somalia. But Clinton consciously changed the nature of the operation, from a U.S.-led humanitarian mission, to one of "nation building" led by the U.N. The Commander-in-Chief who had avoided military service in Vietnam was now eager to commit American lives to war on behalf of the United Nations.

We can still remember the gruesome scenes. A body of an American soldier was dragged through the streets of Mogadishu, Somalia. Supporters of Somali warlord Mohammed Farrah Aidid strapped the corpse of another U.S. soldier to a wheel barrow. Still others waved a bloody limb. This unholy desecration said a lot about the nature of the thugs our troops faced. Unfortunately, the fact that this happened also said a lot about the morally bankrupt Clinton policy that put our troops there. The policy had no defined goals, was compromised by the authority given to the United Nations, and included no timetable for withdrawal.

The U.S./U.N. mission in Somalia ended in a humiliating

withdrawal because it was compromised from the start. In a mission that resembles current NATO operations in Bosnia designed to apprehend suspected "war criminals," U.S. Army Rangers in Somalia were ordered to capture General Aidid. A 15-hour firefight resulted in 18 Americans dead and 84 wounded. In this battle, it took hours for U.N. headquarters to get needed supplies and reinforcements to the Americans. Secretary of Defense Les Aspin had also withheld needed equipment and supplies from our forces.

The Somalia disaster can never be forgotten. It represented Clinton's first attempt to order our troops on a U.N. mission. The Somalia disaster, in part, caused Clinton and his backers to switch gears, to slow the process of using the U.N. itself as a world army. When the next intervention took place, in Haiti, U.S. troops were used only under U.N. authorization – but not direct U.N. control – to install a pro-Communist ruler, Jean-Bertrande Aristide. U.S. troops were deployed on behalf of the U.N. to overthrow one government and install another. From the U.N. viewpoint, however, this was "nation-building" at its best. This deployment was not unprecedented. The same type of deployment, with similar results, was utilized in the Congo in the 1960's to prop up the Communist puppet Patrice Lumumba.

The policy had been laid out in advance in Mandate for Change, the book expressing the views of the Democratic Leadership Council (DLC) and its think tank, the Progressive Policy Institute. President Clinton had served as a chairman of the DLC. Other chairmen included Senators Sam Nunn and Charles Robb, and Representative Richard Gephardt. Vice President Al Gore was a DLC member when he was in the U.S. Senate.

Mandate for Change presented a foreign policy that put heavy emphasis on the U.N. In a chapter entitled, "U.S. Global Leadership for Democracy," Will Marshall strongly endorsed

U.S. involvement in U.N. military operations, saying:

"The U.S. should support the creation of a United Nations rapid-deployment force that could take on policing and relief duties that might otherwise fall into our lap by default....This would not require the U.N. to maintain a large standing army, but rather a force that could be called up from units of national armed forces — including our own — and earmarked and trained in advance."[5]

The clear intention was to create an environment under which American forces were to be placed under U.N. command or authorization. Some analysts contend that American troops have served temporarily under foreign commanders in the past, including U.N. commanders. But today's circumstances are radically different. One difference is that Clinton ordered some of them to wear U.N. uniforms. Another critical difference is that the Clinton Administration clearly coordinated its efforts with U.N. plans to activate Article 43 of the U.N. Charter, which authorizes a standing U.N. force. The Administration's action had to be understood in the context of what U.N. Secretary General Boutros Boutros-Ghali had openly proclaimed in his so-called "Agenda for Peace" report of January 31, 1992. He explained:

"Under Article 42 of the (U.N.) Charter, the Security Council has the authority to take military action to maintain or restore international peace and security. While such action should only be taken when all peaceful means have failed, the option of taking it is essential to the credibility of the United Nations as a guarantor of international security. This will require bringing into being, through negotiations, the special agreements foreseen in Article 43 of the Charter, whereby Member States undertake to make armed forces, assistance and facilities available to the Security Council for the purposes stated in Article 42, not only on an ad hoc basis but on a permanent basis."

---

[5] Will Marshall and Martin Schram, <u>Mandate for Change</u> (New York: Berkeley Books, 1993), p. 306.

President Clinton's selection of General John M. Shalikashvili, the NATO Commander, to succeed General Colin Powell as chairman of the U.S. Joint Chiefs of Staff, was designed to further this policy. Journalist Fred Barnes had reported that in June, 1993, General Shalikashvili had endorsed the expansion of the U.N. in military affairs, with NATO playing an auxiliary role. This is exactly, of course, what has come about. The General was quoted as saying, "NATO should not be viewed as a tool of the United Nations, but rather as a partner where the United Nations establishes the moral and legal mandate for specific action and the Alliance (NATO) provides the tools, or at least the majority of the tools, to fulfill that mandate."[6]

Another clear indication of Administration intent was the decision to appoint the controversial Morton Halperin to a new post in the Department of Defense as Assistant Secretary of Defense for Democracy and Peacekeeping. Halperin had written that "The United States should explicitly surrender the right to intervene unilaterally in the internal affairs of other countries by overt military means or by covert operations. Such self-restraint would bar interventions like those in Grenada or Panama unless the United States first gained the explicit consent of the international community acting through the (U.N.) Security Council or a regional organization."[7]

Ironically, Halperin's pro-U.N. views proved to be some of the least controversial that he held. Much of the criticism of his nomination focused on his support of the pro-Communist CIA turncoat, Philip Agee. He was so controversial that the U.S. Senate failed to confirm him. President Clinton turned around and named him to a staff position on the National Security Council, a post that didn't require Senate confirmation.

Before Clinton, President John F. Kennedy had pushed the concept of a U.N. "peace force" that would replace the armies

---

[6] Boutros Boutros-Ghali, "An Agenda for Peace," report of the Secretary-General pursuant to the statement adopted by the Summit Meeting of the Security Council on 31 January 1992 (New York: United Nations, 1992), p. 25.
[7] As quoted by Senator Paul Coverdell, "Charting a Clear Foreign Policy Course," Washington Times, January 4, 1994, p. A14.

of the nation states. It was spelled out in a State Department document entitled, "Freedom from War: The United States Program for General and Complete Disarmament." Also known as Publication 7277, it urged the "disbanding of all national armed forces and the prohibition of their reestablishment in any form whatsoever other than those required to preserve internal order and for contributions to a United Nations peace force."

The plan has not yet been completed. However, in a July 16, 1992 letter, a State Department "foreign affairs specialist" informed a member of the public that "many of the specific arms control proposals" outlined in that and a related document "have been achieved or are presently being negotiated." He described a number of areas dealing with arms-control treaties.[8]

The one area where Clinton appeared to buck the U.N. planners came when the U.S. initially decided not to sign a treaty designed to "ban" landmines that came out of a December 1997 U.N. conference. A Pentagon study had warned that such a ban would result in at least 35 percent more American causalities in a war. However, in May, 1998, Clinton reversed course, announcing that the U.S. would join the treaty by the year 2006, regardless of whether the U.S. has developed replacements for the mines or not. Former Assistant Secretary of Defense Frank Gaffney commented, "President Clinton has once again demonstrated his willingness to disregard the best interests of the U.S. military - and to put its men and women needlessly at risk."

In his autobiography, <u>An American Life</u>, the true feelings of disdain that President Reagan had for the U.N. came through in a section dealing with the organization's role in the Cold War. In 1986, after the U.S. arrested a Soviet spy in the U.S, Soviet KGB agents seized and imprisoned a Moscow correspondent for U.S. News & World Report, Nicholas Daniloff,

---

[8] Matthew Murphy, Foreign Affairs specialist, Department of State, letter, July 16, 1992.

and accused him of spying for the U.S. The trumped-up charges against Daniloff angered Reagan, who recognized the arrest of Daniloff as a typical Soviet ploy to grab an innocent American and then offer him in exchange for the apprehended Soviet agent.

In retaliation, in a September 9 entry in his personal diary, Reagan proposed that we "kick a half hundred of their UN KGB agents out of the country." The number, though, dwindled down to 25. "We're sending 25 of their UN staff home," Reagan wrote. "All are KGB agents." When the Secretary General of the U.N. stated that the U.S. eviction of the Soviets was against the U.N. charter, Reagan commented, "He'd better be careful, if we cut off [their] UN allowance they might be out of business."[9] Reagan's reaction reflects the fact that, from its inception, the U.N. has consistently sided with the Communists. It's a tragedy that this attitude was not reflected in some of the key appointments he made in the foreign policy and military arena.

Echoing Reagan, John R. Bolton, assistant secretary of state for international organization affairs during the Bush Administration, points out that the U.N. failed to play a positive role in "the most profound and dangerous regional standoff" during the 40 years of the Cold War – the division of Europe. "There," he said, "the U.N. was missing in action." Indeed, the U.N. was "missing in action" from our side, but it played an active role on the Soviet side.

In 1993, at a summit in Vancouver, President Clinton and Russian President Boris Yeltsin announced the establishment of a "strategic partnership" between the two countries that involved military cooperation. At the conclusion of a September 8 Pentagon ceremony, where a "Memorandum of Understanding" was signed by then Defense Secretary Les Aspin and Russian Defense Minister Pavel Grachev, Aspin said that, "Following President Clinton's direction, I have

[9] Matthew Murphy, Foreign Affairs specialist, Department of State, letter, July 16, 1992.

made building this partnership a top priority." He said, "It is a partnership in which military and defense relations play a leading role."[10]

Aspin explained:

"It is an agreement that recognizes that the well-being and the security of the United States and the Russian Federation are vitally related. It is an agreement that seeks to put the years of superpower rivalry and nuclear confrontation behind us. And it is an agreement that builds for the future by formally establishing a series of continuing contacts and relationships between our two defense establishments."[11]

The initiatives in the memorandum included a peacekeeping exercise involving military forces from both countries. The exercise, dubbed "Peacekeeping 94" and featuring 250 U.S. and 250 Russian infantry soldiers, was carried out in September of 1994 in Russia. The Americans used Russian helicopters and armored personnel carriers because they were not allowed to bring their own equipment. A joint exercise was held in the U.S. the following year.

Significantly, the idea of U.S.-Russian peacekeeping exercises was an idea proposed by Grachev. The Washington Post even reported, "One official said Aspin welcomed the idea enthusiastically, adding that there is a real prospect that Russians or Americans might operate one day under the command of their former chief adversary."[12]

How might U.S. forces be commanded by Russians? The U.N. provides the answer.

President Clinton's "Policy on Reforming Multilateral Peace Operations," the public version of Presidential Decision Directive 25, included this curious paragraph:

[10] Media Availability With Les Aspin, U.S. Secretary of Defense, and General of the Army Pavel Grachev, Russian Minister of Defense, The Pentagon, Arlington, Virginia, Defense Department Briefing, September 8, 1993.
[11] Barton Gellman, "Brothers-in Arms: Now GI Joe and Ivan to Train Together," The Washington Post, September 9, 1993, p.A1.
[12] Quoted in "Clinton's U.N. Peacekeeping Plan Still Flawed," Republican Research Committee, Undated., p.3

"With respect to the question of peacekeeping in the territory of the former Soviet Union, requests for traditional UN blue-helmeted operations will be considered on the same basis as other requests."[13]

An analysis of this document noted that the use of the phrase "territory of the former Soviet Union" implied an Eastern Europe "still defined in terms of Russian imperialism rather than by the establishment of independent states."[14] It suggested that U.N. troops could be deployed at Russia's request to reassert Russian control over the "former" Soviet Union.

It didn't take long until a version of this came to pass. On July 22, 1994, the U.N. Security Council approved a resolution "welcoming Russia's contribution to a peacekeeping force in Abkhazia," a region of Georgia. The Russian Ambassador to the U.N., Yuli Vorontsov, had said that without U.N. acceptance of Russian peacekeeping in Georgia, Moscow would veto a U.N. resolution authorizing an invasion of Haiti. Washington Post foreign affairs columnist Lally Weymouth called it a "cynical deal," noting that "the United States has given Russia the right to reoccupy the Caucasus and other former Soviet republics in return for Russian acquiescence in U.N. Security Council resolutions on Haiti." But Weymouth also saw the whole exercise as a violation of the U.N.'s own rules:

"In supporting, albeit tacitly, Russian 'peacekeeping' in Georgia, the United States appears to have redefined the U.N. peace-keeping mandate. For example, under the U.N. Charter, no more than one-third of a peace-keeping force can come from any one country. But the 'peace-keepers' in Georgia are almost exclusively Russian."[15]

With the Clinton Administration in power – and a cooperative Republican Congress – U.S. and Russian troops, with

---

[13] Lally Weymouth, "Yalta II," The Washington Post, July 24, 1994, p.C7.
[14] This document could be found, at the time we were writing this book, on the internet at: http//www/un.org/Depts/dda/Firstcom/SGreport52/a52298.html
[15] Tanya K. Metaksa, Executive Director, NRA Institute for Legislative Action, NRA letter, July 1998.

U.N. backing and assistance, were deployed together as members of the peacekeeping force in Bosnia. There is no end to this deployment in sight. And the prospect that Russians could command U.S. troops remains a distinct possibility.

Unanswered Questions

One question looms large – a question posed to American Marines in Lt. Commander Guy Cunningham's survey – as to whether American soldiers on a U.N. mission would open fire on their fellow Americans resisting confiscation of their firearms. Could this mercenary army be used against American citizens? Cunningham's survey found that about twenty-five percent of our troops said they would shoot Americans if ordered to do so – a shocking finding. The day will come when this question must be answered.

All this at the same time the U.N. is engaged in negotiations aimed at an international gun-ban treaty. Americans can argue with the International Criminal Court about the Second Amendment all they like, it will do no good.

An August 27, 1997 U.N. General Assembly document, "General and Complete Disarmament: Small Arms," includes proposals that could strike at the very heart of our own Second Amendment freedoms. It urges global scrutiny of everything from clubs and knives to revolvers and hunting weapons.[16]

Lawrence Pratt, executive director of Gun Owners of America, says U.S. documents make it clear "they are very serous about disarming American civilians." He cites U.N. surveys and various projects on the issue of "civilian disarmament."

The National Rifle Association says proposals developed by one U.N. body, the U.N. Crime Prevention and Criminal Justice Commission, include:

Limiting gun ownership to one gun per person.

Forcing hunters to remove their guns from their

---

[16] Security Council press release, "Security Council Encourages States to Make Trained Civilian Police Available At Short Notice for United Nations Operations," July 14, 1997.

homes and store them only at sporting clubs.

Requiring private citizens to prove you 'need' a gun, and to obtain official government permission before you can own one.

Requiring expensive insurance for all gun owners.

Forcing firearms collectors to render all their guns non-functional.

Placing an upper age limit on gun ownership. That means once you reach a certain age, you must hand over your gun to the government."[17]

As the U.N. develops a world army capable of enforcing a global gun-ban, it is also working to develop its own police force capable of monitoring and enforcing such a ban. In Bosnia, as noted, an "International Police Task Force" was created, under the control of the U.N. Secretary-General. In July 1997, in noting the "increasing role and special functions of civilian police" in U.N. peacekeeping operations, the U.N. Security Council issued a statement to "encourage States to make available to the United Nations at short notice appropriately trained civilian police" through special arrangements with the U.N. for other deployments.[18]

The first test may come in Albania, where the New York Times reported that the government had asked the U.N. "to help disarm a civilian population that has amassed hundreds of thousands of weapons and a vast supply of ammunition..." The U.N. Undersecretary-General for disarmament affairs agreed that the U.N. would supervise the effort.[19]

But U.S. troops already played that role in Somalia, with disastrous results. Many forget that the U.N. Security Council on March 26, 1993 had passed a resolution emphasizing "the crucial importance of disarmament," including maintaining

[17] Barbara Crossette, "U.N. Agrees to Help Albanian Government Disarm Civilians," New York Times, July 14, 1998.
[18] Memorandum for Senator Thurmond and Senator Nunn. Review of the Circumstances Surrounding the Ranger Raid on October 3-4, 1993 in Mogadishu, Somalia, September 29, 1995, p.14.
[19] Barbara Crossette, "U.N. Agrees to Help Albanian Government Disarm Civilians," New York Times, July 14, 1998.

control of the "heavy weapons" of the organized factions until they are brought under "international control," and the seizure of the "small arms of all unauthorized armed elements and to assist in the registration and security of such arms..."[20]

Just a few months later, in August, 18 members of the Ranger Task Force were killed and 84 were wounded in a raid against the faction led by General Aidid.

Could something like this happen in America? Michael pegged it instinctively when he said, "Dad, if they can make me wear that uniform in Europe, they can make me wear it in Texas."

Such questions are possible because it is apparent that the U.N. is pursuing a policy that aims to disarm the "factions" of the entire world, including nation-states, to such an extent that the U.N. becomes the predominant military power.

Clinton is pursuing this policy for the time being through NATO. But he has still not given up on the idea of an official standing U.N. Army. George Archibald of the Washington Times disclosed that the Clinton Administration was secretly funding the establishment of a "standby" U.N. army. "Congressional officials are investigating $200,000 the Clinton Administration gave the United Nations last fall to mobilize a worldwide standby army for peacekeeping operations," he reported. The money, taken from American taxpayers, went to create a U.N. trust fund to finance a new U.N. military operation called the Rapidly Deployable Mission Headquarters. Archibald said the administration gave "back door" support to the scheme because of the "political sensitivity" over creating a standing U.N. army.

However, the differences between a "standby" and "standing" army are few. A standby army involves different countries providing troops to the U.N. A standing army involves troops directly under U.N. control. In either case, the U.N. would be able to directly call on potentially tens of thousands

---

[20] Memorandum for Senator Thurmond and Senator Nunn. Review of the Circumstances Surrounding the Ranger Raid on October 3-4, 1993 in Mogadishu, Somalia, September 29, 1995, p.14

of troops for "peacekeeping" missions. In the case of the U.N. "standby" army, the administration decided to "reprogram" foreign aid money intended for another purpose into the U.N.

This was finally too much for Congress to take. Rep. Joel Hefley (R-CO) went on the House floor on May 20, 1998 to introduce a resolution cutting off U.S. funds to the stand-by U.N. Army. His measure passed by a vote of 250-172. The vote was a sign of hope that the U.N.'s plans for a mercenary army could eventually be turned back. But it will take a lot of public pressure and a Congress with a backbone. Much more work has to be done.

Conservatives have historically tended to be very pro-military, with or without a Constitutional underpinning for their position. Selective Service is a case in point. In a free republic, where involuntary servitude is forbidden under the Constitution, how does the government justify forcing its citizens to participate in war? Conservatives have traditionally supported this position. But now that we can see the draft being applied to our sons – and our daughters(!) – to impress them into service under the United Nations against their will, now the light of Constitutionality may suddenly dawn upon many more parents.

When a war is not popular back home, perhaps it's an indication that the country ought not be involved in it. If you "have a war, and nobody comes," as the peaceniks used to say, then perhaps you ought to reconsider. Whereas, if our borders are invaded, no one doubts that America will respond and meet the invaders at the beaches. A defensive war never needs a draft to force people to defend their country. What other kind of war is justifiable?

Every time I read the concerns of the Founding Fathers in the Declaration of Independence and the Constitution about the dangers of a standing army in times of peace, the more I wonder when America will recognize the need for us to reduce our army to an officers' corps, returning our troops to the respective states and national guards, and calling upon them only when Congress sees the need to declare war. This is not a plea for our nation to be weak, militarily. Technology makes it easier than ever to defend ourselves from attack today. A standing army grows soft and restless and must be employed, legally or otherwise. Sending our army back to the States could greatly reduce the temptation of presidents to turn them into mercenaries. Furthermore, it may well generate among the governors of the nation a more proper concern for the protection of the lives of the citizens of each state.

In the meantime, we're now in the process of realizing the fulfillment of George Orwell's prophecy that our masters must have "perpetual war for perpetual peace." If there's not an enemy, if there's not a crisis, then one must be manufactured, in order that the nations may be galvanized into action. And that action always seems to result in centralization of power toward the State, the Nation and the United Nations.

Chapter 5

War Crimes:
The International Criminal Court

★★★★

"America goes not abroad in search of monsters to destroy. She well knows that by once enlisting under other banners than her own, were they even banners of foreign independence, she would involve herself, beyond the powers of extrication, in all the wars of interest and intrigue, of individual avarice, envy, and ambition which assume the colors and usurp the standard of freedom. She might become the dictatress of the world; she would no longer be the ruler of her own spirit."
—John Quincy Adams, July 4, 1821

Michael New was prosecuted for refusing to serve in the U.N.'s growing mercenary army. Ironically, if he had stayed in the service – either as an American or a U.N. soldier – he could conceivably be prosecuted today on another charge: "war crimes."

I have been explaining to audiences for some time that there are but three legs of the stool remaining to make a one-world government possible, and one of those legs is a World Court. There must be some agency to arbitrate disputes, and every government requires a Judiciary branch.

The other two legs, of course, are a World Tax and a World Army to enforce the orders of the court, to collect the taxes, and to impose the will of the central government upon the world.

Every administration since Franklin Roosevelt has increased this nation's commitment to the "international community." Harry Truman called it a "bipartisan foreign policy."

While Democrats tend to be more aggressive in this field, a case can be made for regarding George Bush as our greatest Globalist since Roosevelt.[1] Today, the Clinton-Gore administration has put our soldiers into an increasingly untenable situation. As more of them have been deployed around the world, mostly on behalf of the U.N., they stand more chances of being prosecuted – by the U.N. itself!

This was dramatically demonstrated when a U.N. conference recently voted overwhelmingly for a treaty to create an International Criminal Court (ICC) that could prosecute American citizens, including our troops.[2] The ICC claims the right to prosecute Americans before a foreign tribunal without the Constitutional protections of our Bill of Rights. The Washington Times noted, "The court's statute effectively gives it authority over every nation in the world, including those that refuse to ratify it. That means that even without American consent, U.S. soldiers could still be called before the court on accusations of war crimes, crimes against humanity, genocide, or aggression."[3]

David Scheffer, the U.S. ambassador-at-large for war-crimes issues and our main representative at the U.N. negotiating the ICC, had gone into the conference prepared to put Americans under the jurisdiction of the ICC. He had said, "It is not credible to argue that the United States is supporting the creation of this court while guaranteeing that no American will ever come before it. We are not saying Americans are off bounds."[4] However, when the U.N. voted to do just that, he balked. The Clinton-Gore Administration voted against the final draft, but only because they were insisting on a veto power for the members of the Security Council.

[1] Ironically, when I made a statement along this line to a reporter, indicating my opinion that this problem is not to be found in just the Democratic Party, Mr. Bush's press aide sent me a personal letter stating, "I was deeply offended by your quote on the front page of yesterday's *Wall Street Journal* suggesting President Bush somehow supports the subjugation of American sovereignty. Nothing could be further from the truth." Perhaps a chapter in my next book can deal with Mr. Bush's long record of internationalism, but even that would be inadequate.
[2] In Rome, July 17, 1998.
[3] Betsy Pisik, "World criminal court created," *The Washington Times*, July 18, 1998, p.1.
[4] Quoted in "U.S. may nix plan for U.N. tribunal," Betsy Pisik, *The Washington Times*, October 22, 1997, p. 1.

However, all Americans, including civilians, are now potential targets of the ICC. The 120-7 vote for the treaty by various nations of the world amounted to a declaration of war on our rights as American citizens. If allowed to take effect, it constitutes nothing less than a bloodless coup de'etat, a conquest by declaration. It means the Globalists move into the final phase of eliminating national sovereignty.

The significance of the development of the ICC cannot be underestimated. In a continuing quest for the powers that would make it into a full-fledged world state, the United Nations has now claimed the authority to arrest, prosecute and imprison people on a world-wide basis.

The alleged crimes to be prosecuted by the ICC include genocide, crimes against humanity, war crimes and "aggression," which wasn't defined. But under the treaty, one can be guilty of genocide for causing "serious bodily or mental harm to members of the group…." One can be guilty of war crimes for "willfully causing great suffering, or serious injury to body or health...," or of "committing outrages upon personal dignity, in particular humiliating and degrading treatment…." Thus, making people feel bad is grounds for prosecution. Perhaps we need to be much more careful about our ethnic jokes.

The Clinton Administration backed away from supporting the ICC. Was it because this administration favors national sovereignty and could see that our independence is directly threatened by the existence of the International Criminal Court? Hardly.

The Clinton hesitation is because the administration wanted an exemption for U.S. troops – not necessarily those acting to protect and defend our own national security interests – but those serving as "peacekeepers" or picking up "war criminals" in foreign countries.

Any modicum of independence has become too much for the U.N. General Assembly and its various conferences to tol-

erate. The pack of third-world countries, many of which are little more than glorified tribal dictatorships propped up with
American foreign aid and United Nations recognition, are now
smelling blood. This anti-American bias, which has always
been a lurking force in the U.N. general assembly, and even
more so in its world-wide bureaucracy, is now rising to the top,
as the USA gradually reduces its restraining hand and gives the
pack more leeway to howl and demand that America be
brought to its knees. These little banana republics and family-
run governments represent their citizens even less than Bill
Clinton represents the American people. Their desire for power
is normal. What is abnormal is for a powerful country to abdi-
cate, to voluntarily turn that power over to others, and even
worse, to turn it over to those who do not share our cultural and
historical world view. There is a word for such activities.

Notice the words of State Department spokesman James
Rubin in explaining why the Clinton Administration decided
not to support the ICC. He did not say that members of the
U.S. Armed Forces could be prosecuted. He said that "peacekeepers" could be prosecuted. Further, Rubin said the ICC
"could inhibit the ability of the United States to meet alliance
[NATO] obligations and participate in multinational peacekeeping operations." Consider that he said absolutely nothing
about inhibiting the ability of our troops to defend America's
national security interests. That's because national interests
have been subjugated to international interests by this administration. Opposition to the ICC was explained totally in terms
of U.S. participation in U.N.-style military operations.[5] And
who are these peacekeepers? They are our own troops, under
the authority of NATO and the United Nations.

USA Today reported, "The USA said its chief concern was
that U.S. soldiers stationed abroad as peacekeepers could be
charged with crimes such as rape or torture without U.S. consent, even if Washington does not sign the agreement."[6]

---

[5] George Gedda, "U.S. Opposes War Crimes Tribunal," Associated Press, July 20, 1998.
[6] Barbara Slavin, "Jurisdiction worry puts U.S. off court pact," *USA Today*, July 23, 1998, p. 5a.

Again, note the term "peacekeepers."

Even the Pentagon has taken this position. As noted by the *New York Times* in a dispatch before the U.N. conference, the Pentagon had issued a memorandum warning that "if the court was set up and was not properly restrained, it could target their own soldiers – particularly when they were acting as peacekeepers - and subject them to frivolous or politically motivated investigations by a rogue prosecutor or an overzealous tribunal."[7]

This memorandum was distributed to more than 100 foreign military attaches from embassies in Washington, D.C. It had no significant impact, as demonstrated by the 120-7 vote for the ICC treaty and against the U.S. position. Nevertheless, the memorandum serves to demonstrate current thinking in the Department of Defense. This document, which reflects the views of top Clinton-appointed officials, included the following important and controversial statements:

> "The U.S. is committed to replace the ad hoc approach to international war crimes tribunals with a standing court that can address future Cambodias or Yugoslavias.

> "The U.S. is committed to the successful establishment of a court.

> "There should be an appropriate role in the exercise of ICC jurisdiction for the UN Security Council, on which the members of the United Nations have conferred primary responsibility for the maintenance of international peace and security..."

Using pro-U.N. terminology, the Pentagon was supporting the establishment of an ICC – the same position as the Clinton-Gore Administration – as long as the Security Council, where the U.S. has a permanent seat and a veto, had a role in approving or blocking prosecutions. It was actually a

[7] Eric Schmitt, "Pentagon Battles Plans for International War Crimes Tribunal," *New York Times*, April 14, 1998

variation of the position held by Senator Jesse Helms (R-N.C.), chairman of the Senate Foreign Relations Committee, who was depicted as a strong opponent of the ICC but had actually said he would consider ratification of the treaty as long as it contained a U.S. veto. According to a release from Senator Helms' office, he had warned that any treaty establishing an ICC "without a clear U.S. veto...will be dead-on-arrival" at his committee.[8]

But a U.S. veto would be exercised by the executive branch, not by Congress, and it's not at all clear that a liberal president like Bill Clinton or Al Gore would veto the prosecution of an American soldier like Michael New. So the Helms position was questionable from the standpoint of preventing Americans from coming under the jurisdiction of this court.

This is not unlike wife-swapping. When the topic comes up, and you allow yourself to engage in arguing the details, then you're already in trouble. The exclusivity of your marriage is at an end, and it really doesn't matter how vociferously you debate the details.

I will go further and say, categorically, that any American who does so is a traitor. The real veto is, in fact, in the U.S. Constitution. The Constitution says the judicial power rests with the Supreme Court and inferior courts. There is no authority to render the "Supreme" Court an inferior court. There is no loophole to create an ICC with or without a veto. There is no way under the Constitution that an American could or should come before this tribunal. Indeed, there is no basis under the Constitution for even negotiating American participation in such a court.

Senator John Ashcroft (R-Mo.) took a Constitutional position, noting that the Administration went into the negotiations with no insistence that the ICC incorporate and honor the Bill of Rights. "America's position as the world leader is, in no small part, a product of the Constitution that is the envy of the

---

[8] News release, "Helms Declares U.N. Criminal Court 'Dead-On-Arrival' In Senate Without U.S. Veto," March 26, 1998.

world. The Administration should be justly proud of our Constitution and should insist upon it as the starting point for any negotiations of an ICC."[9] This position would have doomed the ICC from the start, because most of the nations at the U.N. never would have accepted it. The ICC conference might never have occurred, and if it had, the United States would not have been represented.

Cliff Kincaid, President of **America's Survival**, was the chief organizer of the **Coalition for American Sovereignty and the Bill of Rights**, which staged a news conference on June 12, 1998, with Senator Ashcroft to oppose the ICC. Kincaid, who was introduced by Senator Ashcroft, assembled a coalition of more than fifty different organizations, including our own Michael New Action Fund.

Speakers at the news conference included former Attorney General Edwin Meese; former Ambassador Frank Ruddy; Center for Security Policy director Frank Gaffney, a former Assistant Secretary of Defense; Michael Boos, director of the National Citizens Legal Network, and Lee Casey of Hunton & Williams, the co-author of an article in *Commentary* magazine attacking the ICC. The coalition's advisory board included John Bolton of the American Enterprise Institute, a former Assistant Secretary of State, and Ted Carpenter of the Cato Institute.

The mission of the coalition was three-fold:

- to support American sovereignty
- to support the constitutional rights of all Americans
- to oppose civil rights violations by an International Criminal Court or any other global body or institution.

During the first week of the ICC conference, Kincaid appeared on the C-SPAN television network to debate the ICC

[9] News release, "Ashcroft, New Coalition Exposes Dangers of World Criminal Court," June 12, 1998.

issue with Stephen Rickard of Amnesty International. He denounced the treaty as unconstitutional and pointed out that Rickard's group is part of a pro-ICC coalition run by the World Federalist Movement (WFM), an organization dedicated to world government. The WFM played the key role in the NGO Coalition for an International Criminal Court. William R. Pace, the "convenor" of the NGO Coalition, is the executive director of the WFM, and the NGO Coalition's mailing address is the same as the WFM. Steven Gerber, a staffer from the World Federalist Association (WFA), the U.S. affiliate, has served as the coordinator of the Washington Working Group on the International Criminal Court.

The WFM views the ICC as only one element of an emerging "world federation" or "world government" that will result from a strengthening of the United Nations.[10] It says this new world system should have "adequate sources of revenue" (i.e. global taxes); a "world peacekeeping force;" a "World Disarmament Authority;" and a "world federal constitution."[11]

The WFA says that through the addition of new global institutions such as the ICC **"national sovereignty would be gradually eroded until it is no longer an issue"** and that a world federation will be formally adopted "with little resistance." (Emphasis mine.)

The WFA has attracted the support of several prominent political figures and personalities, such as John B. Anderson, the former Republican Congressman and 1980 independent U.S. presidential candidate, who serves as WFA president; and former CBS News anchorman Walter Cronkite.

The WFM/WFA also has high-level government contacts. In 1993, Clinton State Department official Strobe Talbott received the "Global Governance Award" from the WFA. In a letter praising WFA and Talbott, President Clinton noted that Norman Cousins, a founder of the WFA, "worked for

---

[10] See the WFM site on the Internet: (www.getnet.com/wfa/intl.htm).
[11] Ibid.

world peace and world government." Clinton wished the WFA "future success."

While the Pentagon did not join the WFM/WFA in actually endorsing the ICC, it stated in its memorandum that the U.S. had "provided important resources and personnel in support of the Bosnia and Rwanda war crimes tribunals."

This was true, unfortunate, and tragic. These tribunals are stepping stones to the ICC. And the ICC is one of the keys to a One World Government.

In one such case of "global justice," in a preview of what the ICC could do to Americans, a war crimes "suspect" being held in a United Nations prison cell in the Netherlands by the Bosnia tribunal was found dead – "hanged" – in a case of alleged "suicide" on June 29, 1998. The dead "suspect," Slavko Dokmanovic, the former Serb Mayor of Vukovar, had been invited by a U.N. official under false pretenses to a meeting, where he was seized and handcuffed by about 20 masked gunmen. He was then taken to The Hague, Netherlands, where the tribunal is based, and where he was jailed. In a statement, President Clinton said he welcomed the kidnapping, noting that Dokmanovic was "under sealed indictment," meaning that he had no idea he had been charged with any crime at all.

This kind of fraud and deceit is typical of United Nations' representatives over the past fifty years. It's a slippery slope for governments to openly endorse.

U.N. authorities said he committed suicide because he was depressed about a forthcoming verdict in his case. This may or may not be true. But Washington Post reporter Charles Trueheart said U.N. prosecutors had "failed to muster clear-cut evidence of his active participation" in any killings. So we are supposed to believe that he was depressed over a possible verdict of not guilty? Does this make any sense at all? Equally suspicious, he had been in a locked cell, but the Post's Trueheart said that he had apparently "been able to get the locked cell door open" and hang himself from a door hinge with a piece of cord. It is not clear how or where he got the cord.

Just a few days after this strange incident, the president of the U.N. tribunal which carried out and supervised his imprisonment said that she is proud of the work she has done and that the ICC should operate the same way. Gabrielle Kirk McDonald told the ICC conference in Rome, "I think we've done a good job with our rules."

The problem is that her "rules" include tactics that would make the Soviet KGB and the Nazi Gestapo proud. If President Clinton and Gabrielle McDonald and the Hague can publicly be proud of deceptive and fraudulent negotiations, as well as kidnapping, as well as the blatant violation of national integrity in Bosnia, then what does that bode for you and me, sitting on the other side of the world confident that we are protected by our Constitution and our Bill of Rights? The Bill of Rights is null and void wherever the United Nations operates.

Our soldiers are being used today to apprehend "suspects" wanted by McDonald and her ilk. The Clinton Administration was urging its NATO allies to organize a police force to hunt down alleged war criminals and, by January of 1998, American soldiers in Bosnia were playing that role. In one dramatic incident, they rushed from an unmarked van to seize a suspected war criminal. He was snatched, tied up, and thrown into the van. Earlier, U.S. forces had provided back-up for British troops who killed a war crimes suspect. Clearly, that "defendant" won't be standing trial.

In a startling development, *U.S. News & World Report* disclosed that, for the last year, a U.S. special operations task force had been "conducting one of the broadest covert operations since the Vietnam War" – gathering intelligence on war criminals and seizing them in a series of raids. The cost was estimated at $50 million.[12] However, it was reported that one plan

---

[12] Richard J. Newman, "Hunting War Criminals. The First Account of Secret U.S. missions in Bosnia," *U.S. News & World Report*, July 6, 1998.

to seize a "war criminal" was compromised by a female French officer. A French Army major was accused of leaking information about another plan. The magazine said that a "climate of mistrust among NATO allies" had inhibited these efforts.

The *New York Times* disclosed on July 26, 1998, that the National Security Agency, which conducts electronic eavesdropping, the CIA, FBI agents, U.S. Marshals, and NATO had worked together in an effort to locate and apprehend two political and military leaders of the Bosnian Serbs. After spending more than two years and as much as $100 million, the plans were abandoned because they were not considered practical.[13]

In a controversial case that came before the Yugoslavian tribunal, a Bosnian Serb named Goran Lajic was accused of carrying out atrocities against Muslims and Croats at a specific camp in northwestern Bosnia. He was one member of a group of Serbs indicted on charges of murder and torture. Oddly, in the indictment handed down by Richard J. Goldstone, then-prosecutor of the tribunal, the name of Goran Lajic appears but no specific charges appear next to it.

This case was featured by the Coalition for International Justice (which is supported by the American Bar Association) as an example of how the International Criminal Tribunal for the Former Yugoslavia was doing its job. Lajic had been arrested in Germany in March of 1996 and transported to The Hague, where the tribunal is based. He was arraigned in May and pled innocent, saying he had "never set eyes" on the camp in question.

More than two months later, however, on June 17, 1996, the tribunal issued an order "for the withdrawal of the charges" against Lajic and he was returned to Germany. Without any explanation or apology, the court said it turned out to be a case of mistaken identity.[14]

In another case, British NATO troops snatched Bosnia Serb twin brothers as "war crimes suspects" and took them to The

---

[13] Tim Weiner, "U.S. Cancels Plans For Raid on Bosnia To Capture 2 Serbs," *The New York Times*, July 26, 1998, p.1.
[14] "Tribunal Frees Bosnian Serb," *The Washington Post*, June 18, 1996, p. A10.

Hague, where they were accused of torturing and beating to death Muslim inmates at a prison camp. The two men protested their innocence until tribunal authorities admitted, in a major embarrassment, that it was all a mistake – another case of mistaken identity – and they were sent home with an apology. The brothers, who were apparently beaten during their arrest by NATO troops, announced they would sue the U.N. tribunal.[15]

In a case involving the U.N. criminal tribunal for Rwanda, U.S. FBI agents were used in September 1996 to arrest a Rwandan pastor outside Laredo, Texas, on charges of "crimes against humanity" and genocide. The pastor, Elizaphan Ntakirutimana, had fled Rwanda and had been living with family members in Laredo.

The U.N. court wanted him extradited back to Africa to stand trial on the charges. In a startling development, however, he was released in December, 1997, after spending 14 months in a Laredo jail. U.S. Magistrate Notzon, who had issued the arrest warrant, determined that the extradition request was illegal because the U.S. had never ratified a treaty with the U.N. court.

The judge also found that the evidence for the charges against the pastor was vague and questionable. He found the evidence came from a single affidavit filed by a Belgian police officer working for the tribunal. The affidavit cited several alleged witnesses, none of whom was identified, other than by letters (i.e. A,B,C, etc.). One witness was interviewed on multiple occasions. Only one witness actually claimed the pastor participated in an attack on someone. But there was no indication that any of the witnesses were placed under oath prior to making their statements.[16]

Nevertheless, the Bosnia and Rwanda tribunals are said to be models for how the ICC would operate. If so, this is truly

---

[15] "SFOR's mistaken prisoners back in Bosnia, to sue," *Agence France Presse*, July 24, 1998.
[16] See "Memorandum and Order in the Matter of Surrender of Elizaphan Ntakirutimana, In the United States District Court for the Southern District of Texas, Laredo Division," December 17, 1997, pp. 9-11.

frightening. As federal magistrate Notzon discovered, no treaty was ever ratified to create the Yugoslavia court or, for that matter, the Rwanda tribunal. An unofficial document provided by the U.N. Information Office in Washington, D.C. confirms this, saying, "Normally, such a tribunal would be established by treaty rather than by the Security Council. The Secretary-General, however, pointed out that such an approach would require 'considerable time' and that, there could be no guarantee that ratification will be received from those States which should be parties to the treaty if it is to be truly effective.'"

In other words, the Security Council decided to manipulate the U.N. Charter in the name of "global justice." Which is to say that the end justifies the means. The creation of the Yugoslavia and Rwanda courts was itself a power grab which sets a dangerous precedent. It was established without benefit of any treaty by the U.N. Security Council when it decided that Chapter VII of the U.N. Charter, authorizing the deployment of U.N. military forces, also gave the world body the ability to arrest, prosecute and jail individuals.

C. Douglas Lummis, a teacher of political philosophy, has alluded to this, asking, "Where does the U.N. get the power to prosecute individuals?" He points out that the Yugoslavia tribunal "was established by Security Council resolutions, but that answers nothing. Where does the Security Council get such power? The legal fiction is that the power comes from Chapter VII of the U.N. Charter. Chapter VII authorizes the U.N. to deploy the armed forces of member states in peace-keeping operations. Stretch the words as you will, you cannot make them say that the U.N. has the power to put people in jail on criminal charges."[17]

The inevitable conclusion is that the Yugoslavian and Rwandan tribunals are illegal under the "international law" that the U.N. claims to respect. So is an ICC treaty which

[17] C. Douglas Lummis, "Time To Watch the Watchers," *The Nation*, September 26, 1994, pp. 302-306.⁹

claims jurisdiction over countries such as the U.S. which do not ratify it. Which is why Cliff Kincaid reacted to passage of the ICC treaty by declaring that the U.N. "had declared hunting season on Americans." Kincaid noted, "It is claiming the right to prosecute Americans before a foreign tribunal without the Constitutional protections of our Bill of Rights. The vote for the treaty amounts to a declaration of war on our rights as American citizens."

Kincaid went on to say that Congress had several immediate options:

- Termination of foreign aid and other international assistance to any country which signs this treaty
- Refusal to pay a phony financial "debt" to the U.N.
- Hearings into the abuses of currently operating U.N. criminal tribunals in Bosnia and Rwanda, and the defunding of these tribunals
- A flat prohibition on the use of U.S. troops to apprehend "war criminals" wanted by any U.N. tribunal, and
- Congressional Investigations of the NGOs (non-governmental organizations), including the World Federalists, which lobbied behind-the-scenes for the creation of an anti-American ICC.

Kincaid noted, "The creation of this court can only lead to more calls for a complete U.S. withdrawal from the world body. This could serve as a wake-up call to millions of Americans. It could be the death wish of the U.N."

But this is so only if members of Congress seize the opportunity and use the passage of this treaty in a massive educational campaign to tell the truth about the U.N. Why, in short, should the U.S. continue to fund an organization whose members have openly mobilized against us for the purpose of prosecuting our citizens?

Sounding tough, Senator Jesse Helms declared, "The United States must fight this treaty." But he then turned around and advocated a series of new treaties and international agreements designed somehow to protect our troops and citizens from prosecution. This is not the Jesse Helms America once counted on to protect us from globalization.

The Associated Press reported that Helms "promised to seek assurances from Secretary of State Madeleine Albright that all future extradition treaties exempt U.S. citizens from prosecution by the new court and that U.S. soldiers not participate in NATO or U.N. operations until allies agree that the troops would not be subject to the court's jurisdiction." The news service added that, "Helms also said the United States should renegotiate with its allies agreements that govern the operations of U.S. forces deployed abroad and not station American troops in countries that refuse to exempt them from the new court's authority."[18]

Senator Helms' approach fails to challenge the underlying premise of most of these deployments. Why are U.S. troops being deployed as "peacekeepers" under NATO and the U.N. in the first place? The passage of the ICC was an opportunity to begin a radical re-evaluation of U.S. foreign policy and begin the re-deployment or withdrawal of U.S. troops to further the American national security interest. Such a review could lead in increasing calls of "Bring the troops home."

Despite the stated concerns expressed by the Clinton-Gore Administration, it is not likely that the ICC will immediately prosecute U.S. troops operating as U.N. "peacekeepers." It's more likely that the ICC will threaten to prosecute a U.S. military operation which happens to be unpopular with the U.N. Indeed, it could be argued that the ICC is designed to inhibit the U.S. from conducting unilateral military operations except under the authority of the U.N.!

In retrospect, the U.S. bombing of Libya, the U.S. invasion

[18] Joseph Schuman, "US Sens. Fight International Court," Associated Press, July 24, 1998.

of Grenada, and the U.S. invasion of Panama might all qualify as violations of "international law," according to the ICC, because they were not given advance approval by the U.N. American civilian and military leaders who authorized these missions could conceivably be prosecuted by the world body. In addition, U.S. assistance provided to anti-Communist movements in Africa, Central America and Afghanistan during the 1980s could also qualify as "war crimes" or "crimes against humanity."

In the current context, if the U.S. had an Administration which pursued a policy to destabilize the Communist regime in China, this, too, could be construed as a "war crime." Even though China did not sign the ICC treaty, its allies in the "third world" could bring the case against the U.S. anyway. Continued American support for Taiwan, as little and left-handed as it is, could someday become a court case before the ICC.

The concept of using international tribunals to discredit the U.S. is an old ploy used by anti-American countries and movements. With international communist support, Bertrand Russell staged a phony International War Crimes Tribunal in 1967 for the purpose of exposing U.S. "war crimes" in the Vietnam War.

After the conclusion of the Persian Gulf War, the same stunt was pulled by former U.S. Attorney General Ramsey Clark, setting up an "International War Crimes Tribunal" in New York City to press charges, not against Saddam Hussein, but against the U.S. Government and top civilian and military officials, including President George Bush, Vice President Dan Quayle, Joint Chiefs Chairman General Colin Powell, and Secretary of Defense Dick Cheney. They were charged with "high crimes in violation of the Charter of the United Nations [and] international law... ."[19] They were eventually found guilty of those charges by the *ad hoc* "tribunal." The

---

[19] See the International Action Center home page at: http://www.iacenter.org/. You will also find many other interesting extreme left-wing links.

judgment at the time had no force in law. But it may well prove helpful to those who like to operate on precedent.

If it hadn't been for the fact that the U.N. Security Council had endorsed the Persian Gulf War against Saddam Hussein, such a case might well have been brought before and accepted by an official U.N. body. Under the ICC, such cases *will* be brought against the U.S., especially if our troops are deployed on behalf of American national security interests.

As we confront a dangerous future, we have to be aware of a critical fact: our soldiers are currently involved in kidnapping "war criminals." In the future, our own troops or political leaders may be rounded up themselves. It is an unconscionable decision for American soldiers to participate in such activities.

Our challenge as Americans is clear: if we restore our Armed Forces to their rightful place as defenders of American sovereignty and liberty, we might succeed in saving our Constitution and the Bill of Rights. If we fail, it is not only conceivable, it is probable that the International Criminal Court will some day use "its" own troops against us. (And those may turn out to be Americans.) Michael understood this principle instinctively, and it was embodied in his statement very early in his case, "If they can force me to serve the U.N. in Europe, then they can force me to do it in America. Geography is no defense. It's a question of authority."

The challenge is more intense and personal for those U.S. troops who have been ordered into these U.N./NATO operations. They have a decision to make. And they must make it soon. If our elected leaders do not make the right decisions, then it is incumbent upon our military leaders to be loyal to the Constitution and make the right decisions. If they are incapable of doing that, it will become the duty of every individual soldier, marine, sailor and airman to make his or her own personal decision just as Specialist Michael New did.

Used by permission.

Chapter 6

Impeachment

★★★★

"A treaty cannot be made which alters the Constitution of the country, or which infringes any express exceptions to the power of the Constitution."
—*Alexander Hamilton*

> **US Constitution, Article 2, Section 4: "The President, Vice President and all civil Officers of the United States, shall be removed from office on Impeachment for, and Conviction of, Treason, Bribery, or other high Crimes and Misdemeanors."**

Mike Farris, Founder and Director of the Home School Legal Defense Association, recently said the evidence is overwhelming that President Clinton has committed impeachable offenses in Michael New's case.[1] Farris, who was Michael's lead attorney in the first round of appeals in the civilian courts, said "the strongest thing the Congress could do would be to impeach President Clinton." This may be the only way justice in the Michael New case can be secured.

In currently fending off the threat of impeachment, President Clinton is quick to claim the Constitution as his own. In a legal brief attempting to prevent his aides from having to testify about crimes that he, the President, may have committed in the Monica Lewinsky affair, his lawyers argued that he was entitled to a "constitutional protection," and that his "constitutional duties" and "constitutional obligations" required that he be able to obtain certain confidential advice from his advisors. Clinton's lawyers insisted that "constitutional principles" were at stake and that Independent Counsel

---

[1] Speaking at an American Sovereignty Action Project conference on October 22, 1997, in Washington, D.C.

Kenneth Starr had created a "constitutional confrontation."[2]

Impeachment seems to be a viable and reasonable option. The Whitewater allegations of theft and fraud are serious charges. The effort to pressure people to lie regarding President Clinton's relationship with Monica Lewinsky is odious and objectionable. His dealings with Communist China are highly questionable. However, as serious as these are, we believe they don't compare with "violating the sovereignty of the United States, violating specific American laws and criminally prosecuting American troops for only standing up for the Constitution," as Mike Farris put it. "The high stakes are on our sovereignty," he said, "and that to me is an impeachable offense."

The constitutional confrontation already exists, and it is of the President's own making. He violated his oath of office when he tried to make Michael New violate his. The President's oath of office, established in the Constitution itself, consists of the following:

"I do solemnly swear (or affirm) that I will faithfully execute the Office of President of the United States, and will to the best of my ability, preserve, protect and defend the Constitution of the United States."

For those who doubt that Clinton's actions in the Michael New case are illegal and unconstitutional, one can consult the legal briefs that we have assembled on Michael's behalf. However, Senator Mitch McConnell of Kentucky also investigated, and he determined that the deployment to Macedonia in the former Yugoslavia lacks "a clear, legal mandate." In other words, it is illegal. Senator McConnell's comments were inserted into the Congressional Record of September 24, 1996, pages S11173 and S11174. He was prompted to investigate the case by Colonel Ron Ray, a constituent of McConnell's as well as Michael's first defense attorney.

[2] "Advice on an Impeachment Threat 'Is, By Its Very Nature, Official,'" The Washington Post, May 28, 1998, page A17.

Senator McConnell's conclusion still stands as evidence that could be used in articles of impeachment against Clinton.

"For several months," McConnell declared, "I have tried to get a straight answer from the administration on the legal justification for the deployment of U.S. troops under United Nations' command in Macedonia." Eventually, McConnell got a "straight answer" that amounted to the admission that the Clinton administration had violated the law.

"In simple English," McConnell said, "when a Chapter VII mission is authorized by the U.N., U.S. law requires the operation to be approved by Congress. In simple terms, the State Department is using a Chapter VI designation to avoid having to come to the Congress to justify the financial aid and military burden the United States has assumed in Macedonia." We are not alone in believing this is an impeachable offense in and of itself.

McConnell said that Madeleine Albright, then the U.S. Ambassador to the U.N., had claimed during a hearing into the matter that the deployment to Macedonia was a Chapter VI mission under the U.N. Charter and, therefore, didn't require congressional approval. But McConnell said no U.N. Security Council resolutions relating to the former Yugoslavia or Macedonia mentioned a Chapter VI mandate for Macedonia. Instead, 27 different resolutions referred to U.N. operations in the former Yugoslavia as coming under Chapter VII of the U.N. Charter, requiring the explicit approval of the U.S. Congress.

McConnell said he thought the answer to this problem is an amendment to the U.S. law, the U.N. Participation Act of 1949, which governs relations with the U.N. But the real answer is for Congress to hold the administration accountable for a blatant violation of the law and the blatant violation of the U.S. Constitution! This means impeachment.

We need to remind ourselves and our Congressmen that

impeachment is not conviction. It's simply an inquiry into whether a crime has been committed, and if so, then what to do about it. The House of Representatives brings up the articles of impeachment, then the Senate actually conducts the trial. It's a process rarely used in American history, but one that was designed specifically for this type of situation.

I am not simply speaking as a father. All Americans should recognize that it is simply unconscionable that any American soldier can be forced out of the service for objecting to an illegal and unconstitutional order, particularly where national sovereignty is at stake. The constitutional violations occur in several respects.

- The Macedonia mission violates the Constitutional provision in Article I, Section 9, requiring prior congressional approval for acceptance or wearing of foreign badges.

- It's also a violation of the "Appointments Clause" of the Constitution which prevents the president from subjecting American troops to U.N. or any other foreign command without the approval of the U.S. Senate.

- The wearing of the U.N. uniform is also a clear violation of Army regulations, as admitted orally by one of the judges in the Army Court of Criminal Appeals.[3]

In the case of Macedonia, President Clinton is directly responsible for implementing this illegal and unconstitutional policy. As McConnell noted, Clinton himself wrote a letter to Congress in July 1993, stating that the Macedonia mission was a U.N. Chapter VI operation. "But this assertion is not substantiated by the record of resolutions and reports passed by the United Nations," McConnell points out.

The fact is that President Clinton deceived Congress. His purpose was to establish a "precedent" of having American

---

[3] AR 670-1, governing the wear of the Battle Dress Uniform. See appendix.

soldiers transformed into U.N. troops, wearing U.N. uniforms, under U.N. commanders, without Congressional approval. Michael New took a stand. Why won't Congress? Did the President lie deliberately? Far be it from me to make that judgment – it's the job of the Senate to determine that during the impeachment process.

Bill Clinton, who deliberately avoided military service for himself, has now victimized a U.S. Army Specialist whose only "crime" was that he remained true to his oath of allegiance to the U.S. Constitution.

Have we reached the point in America when a draft-dodging "Commander-in-Chief" can successfully engineer the prosecution of a patriotic U.S. soldier, leaving him with a stigma, a bad conduct discharge, which will follow him all the rest of his life? Is this what America has come to represent?

Backing up our legal case, constitutional attorney Lee A. Casey, of the Washington law firm of Hunton & Williams, says the key question is whether the order to Michael was lawful. Since Congress under the Constitution never approved the practice of having a Finnish General run the Macedonia operation, he said, it is unlawful to order New to report to him. He points out that the Finnish officer "does not hold an office created by the Congress of the U.S., and he has not been approved by the president with the advice and consent of the Senate. As a result, he may not exercise military command over American troops. The President cannot allow him to do that and the Congress cannot allow the President to allow him to do that. It cannot be done absent a Constitutional amendment."

PDD 25

In the final analysis, the administration seems to be relying on a secret document, Presidential Decision Directive 25 (PDD 25) for justification of its illegal and unconstitutional policy. This is specifically what Michael was told by his chain of command. However, the Congress, that branch of government constitutionally responsible for declaring war and regulating the Armed Forces, was denied access to this secret pro-U.N. plan, as the following exchange during a May 17, 1994 Congressional hearing illustrates:

> **Rep. Benjamin Gilman**: "Madame Ambassador, on a number of occasions we've requested to see the actual document containing PDD 25. We've gotten some summaries, but thus far we haven't received any full documentation. Can you tell me when we can expect to see the full language of PDD 25?

> **Madeleine Albright**, [then] U.S. Ambassador to the U.N.: "Congressman Gilman, PDD 25 is an executive branch document that is never released to the Congressional side of the government."[4]

Apologists for the administration, such as Representative Tom Lantos (D-Calif.), insisted that the refusal to disclose the actual text of PDD 25 was "standard" procedure by Democratic and Republican Administrations. But the difference was that this was the first ever presidential directive that relinquishes U.S. Government control to an international organization. This concerns a function of government, national defense, in which Congress by law and the Constitution is supposed to play a critical role.

The Constitution clearly gives Congress the power to makes rules and regulations governing the Armed Forces. And it gives NO ONE the power to give away American sovereignty! The word for that, in any dictionary, is "treason." What, if anything, is an impeachable offense?

Despite the failure to release the actual text, the public document was portrayed by the administration and the media as a step backward from the scheme proposed by then-U.N. Secretary-General Boutros Boutros-Ghali for a standing U.N. army. This document flatly stated, "The U.S. does not support a standing U.N. army..." However, one analysis of the proposal noted that,

"...the Clinton plan lays the institutional groundwork for the future creation of such a force by calling for the creation by the U.N. of a Plans Division, an Information and Research Division, an Operations Division, a Logistical Division, a Public Affairs Cell, a Civil Police Cell, and a Professional Peace Operations Training Program. The U.N. should also have a 'rapidly deployable headquarters team' and its own 'modest airlift capabilities.'"[5]

The Clinton Presidential Decision Directive was actually a reformulated version of a proposed Presidential Memorandum Directive 13, whose contents had created a firestorm when the Washington Post revealed some of the details on August 5, 1993. It was immediately withdrawn, only to reappear in a classified version a few months later.

However, the central purpose remained in PDD 25. According to the public version, the document unilaterally affirms the President's authority as Commander-in-Chief "to place U.S. forces under the operational control of a foreign commander when doing so serves American security interests..." However, the document went on to acknowledge that the Administration had not figured out the critical issue of how to protect and defend what it called "U.S. Peacekeepers" – U.S. troops involved in U.N. activities. The document said:

"The U.S. remains concerned that in some cases, captured U.N. peacekeepers and U.N. peace enforcers may not have adequate protection under international law. The U.S. believes that individuals captured while performing U.N. peace keeping or U.N. peace enforcement activities, whether as members of a U.N. force or a U.S. force executing a U.N. Security Council mandate, should, as a matter of policy, be immediately released to U.N. officials; until released, at a minimum, they should be accorded protections

[5] "Clinton's U.N. Peacekeeping Plan Still Flawed," Republican Research Committee, undated.

identical to those afforded prisoners of war under the 1949 Geneva Convention. The U.S. will generally seek to incorporate appropriate language into U.N. Security Council resolutions that establish or extend peace operations in order to provide adequate legal protection to captured U.N. peacekeepers. In appropriate cases, the U.S. would seek assurances that U.S. forces assisting the U.N. are treated as experts on mission for the United Nations, and thus are entitled to appropriate privileges and immunities and are subject to immediate release when captured. Moreover, the Administration is actively involved in negotiating a draft international convention at the United Nations to provide a special international status for individuals serving in peacekeeping and peace enforcement operations under a U.N. mandate. Finally, the Administration will take appropriate steps to ensure that any U.S. military personnel captured while serving as part of a multinational peacekeeping force or peace enforcement effort are immediately released to U.N. authorities."[6]

In effect, the administration was openly acknowledging that U.S. troops assigned to the U.N. become "U.S. Peacekeepers," who are not U.S. POW's or MIA's when captured, and that the U.S. government is under no military obligation to defend them or seek their return. This made PDD 25 into an extraordinary and unprecedented document — an impeachable offense on its face. Through a federal order, William Jefferson Clinton, the man who "loathes the military," has abandoned our soldiers into an international legal twilight zone.

Administration officials had tried to pretend that the policy was nothing new, and that the directive simply reaffirmed the ability of Presidents to temporarily assign U.S. troops to the

---

[6] "The Clinton Administration's Policy on Reforming Multilateral Peace Operations," White House, May 1994. p.2.

operational command of foreigners. Most reporters accep
the administration line. But the issuance of a secret presid
tial directive assigning U.S. troops to a foreign-dominat
organization with a questionable international legal status w;
dangerously different.

Putting the issue in stark and blunt terms, attorney Le
Casey says that if the President has the unilateral power to
order our troops to report to the U.N., he could order them
to report to another government or even a private individual.
As Cliff Kincaid notes in his book, *Global Bondage*, if the
President is granted such power, he could even order our
troops to report to Russian military officers. This prospect is
not so outlandish as it might seem. As noted, President
Clinton's first Secretary of Defense, Les Aspin, actually said
he anticipated the day when Russian military officers might
command our troops. Aspin signed a series of military cooperation agreements with the Russian military which could
bring this about.

In fact, Americans troops engaged in U.N.-style peacekeeping exercises with Russian troops in Russia, and
Russian troops engaged in similar exercises with American
troops at Ft. Riley, Kansas, in 1995.

The same possibility applies to U.S. troops one day being
commanded by Chinese military officers. Under an agreement reached during Clinton's 1998 visit to China, U.S. and
Chinese officials have already worked out a schedule of military exercises that will be observed by the other country.
China sent two observers to watch the six-nation "RimPac"
naval exercises off Hawaii in July and two to watch the five-
nation "Cope Thunder" Air Force exercises in Alaska in
July. Eventually, according to U.S. Special Operations chief
General Peter Schoomaker, Special Forces soldiers will
actually train Chinese Peoples' Liberation Army (PLA)
troops!

the Congress had acted to protect Michael New, we might
be conceiving of the possibility of U.S.-Chinese U.N.-
peacekeeping exercises and the prospect of Russian or
nese military officers commanding U.S. troops. Bill
nton's multinationalism is clearly out-of-control. Our sov-
ignty cannot withstand this kind of assault forever. Will our
urts defend the Constitution? Will Congress defend the
onstitution? What has happened to the system of "checks
and balances" they told us about in government class in high
school?

Remember, the U.S. Constitution does not require clear-cut
evidence that President Clinton has committed serious crimes
before he is impeached for this policy. Senator McConnell's
legal analysis of Michael's case is important, but it is not necessary before proceeding with impeachment. Even if the civilian and military courts ultimately rule on behalf of the
Administration and against Michael, we would still have a
case for impeachment against the President. The Constitution,
after all, refers to impeachment for high crimes and misde-
meanors. These do not denote criminal offenses in the sense
that prosecutors now understand them. Impeachment can be
applied in a case of injury to the state or system of government. Clinton's corrupt pro-U.N. policy has inflicted just such
an injury on our nation.

Military sources agree that there are problems.

It's important for the public to realize that the concern for
what has happened here is not exclusively held by a narrow
segment of the political spectrum. Military people are concerned. For example, read the account of Antje Mays, of The
Citadel, in a paper prepared for presentation to the Joint
Services Conference on Professional Ethics in D.C. in January,
1997, entitled Of Law, Lawlessness, and Sovereignty,[7]

"Confusing command jurisdiction - individual nations under UN command?

---

[7] A paper prepared for presentation to the Joint Services Conference on Professional Ethics XIX,
Washington, D.C. January 30-31, 1997

"Respect for peacekeepers' sovereignty? "A UN-mandated peacekeeping mission was deployed in Macedonia - partially in response to an assassination attempt on its president (& maintain internal stability), partially also to keep the Yugoslavian civil war and its ethnic passions from spreading into Macedonia. In its course, US Army medic Michael New, in his patriotism of serving in the US forces, refused in 1993 to cast off the US insignia to wear the UN emblem and blue helmet. In January 1994 he was court-martialed in Germany, discharged dishonorably on bad-conduct charges, and disqualified from receiving veterans' benefits. This incident over command loyalties sent shockwaves of scandal around the world. Previously, US Congress had introduced a bill which would render US soldiers wearing of UN insignia illegal, and Michael New gained support & sympathy among conservative legislators and military/international law scholars.[8]

"Loyalty disputes between the US and UN were not new to Macedonia: The placement of American troops under often incompetent UN command had endangered US soldiers' lives, procedurally tied their hands, made them appear incompetent themselves, and rendered the US the laughingstock of the world. Images of US soldiers being dragged through the streets of Somalia and their fear of Haitian thugs (due to absence of any UN-approved rights to self defense!!) set a detrimental precedent for the safety of peacekeepers.

"Sovereignty or World Government? More importantly, the legislative implications of this measure are of historic proportions: Presidential Decision Directive 13 (PDD-13)[9] (drafted by the Council on Foreign Relations in 1993)[10] aims to place US troops under UN command. This would turn the UN Secretary General into the technical commander-in-chief of worldwide armed forces which would, of course, be deployed

---

[8] Mays has her dates wrong here. The order was disobeyed in 1995, and the court-martial was in 1996.

[9] It may be that the author is confusing PDD 25 with an earlier Presidential Memorandum Directive #13, on the same topic, but withdrawn from the table.

[10] This is new information to us, and if true, is a bombshell.

under peacekeeping tenets) and relinquish the United States' control over its own soldiers to a multinational administrative body. Where would be the end of possibilities encouraged by such a precedent? Would this set the stage for the end of individual nations' right to self-determination and sovereignty as we know it?

"Of morality, principle, and constitution. We must never forget a nation's moral obligation to protect its own citizens (civilian and military alike) from betrayal to foreign governments and crimes against their freedom and personal dignity. And a government has the absolute constitutional responsibility to uphold its nation's right to self-determination and self-defense.

"Lesson learnt from the Michael New incident? Interestingly, the US troops now being sent to Zaire for humanitarian assistance with the refugees' return to Rwanda are being expressly placed specifically under US command."

Hillary agrees that Bill should be impeached

An "expert" on the subject of impeachment is none other than Hillary Clinton, then known as Hillary Rodham, who served on the staff of the House Judiciary Committee when some members of Congress were threatening the impeachment of President Nixon. "Ms." Rodham helped write a report entitled "Constitutional Grounds for Presidential Impeachment." She makes it clear that impeachment isn't just designed as a remedy for a president who has violated a criminal law. Rather, it is a tool to correct "corruption in office" and was "not necessarily limited to common law or statutory crimes." The report defines this as "serious offenses" by the president which "subvert" our government and "undermine the integrity of office."

Gingrich is protecting Clinton

In moving forward with legislation to begin an inquiry into

the impeachment of President Clinton, Rep. Bob Barr (R-Ga.) has cited Hillary Clinton's work on the subject. His legislation, however, has received relatively few co-sponsors, a problem he has attributed to House Speaker Newt Gingrich (R-Ga.). If Newt wasn't sitting so hard on this, we'd have 200 co-sponsors — not 20," he said last February.[11]

It is important to note that Barr's legislation was introduced before the Monica Lewinsky scandal broke. While one can clearly make a case for impeachment of this president on the misdemeanor grounds of not being able to keep his pants zipped, it might be wiser to consider impeachment on grounds involving our national security and sovereignty. Michael New's case is an important element here. In fact, however, it can be argued that Clinton's overall treatment of the U.S. military in general constitutes a series of impeachable offenses.

From the start of his first term, it seemed that his mission, perhaps a life-long mission, was to radically restructure the American military establishment. Clinton's objectives were to re-engineer the military through massive budget cuts, to admit open homosexuals, to place women on the front lines of combat, and to subordinate American interests to those of the United Nations. Today, most of these objectives have been virtually accomplished.

While to some extent, the subordination of the American military to the International Community has been slowed down by Michael New's case, it is imperative that the American people recognize that the Internationalists in Washington and New York are accomplishing much the same objective via the reformed and redirected NATO currently operating in Europe.

The gutting of America's superior national defense is scandalous and flouts the U.S. Constitution. According to America's founding document, national defense is a mandated obligation of the federal government. Traditionally, this has

[11] Lloyd Grove, "Clinton's Public Enemy," The Washington Post, February 10, 1998, p.E1.

meant that Congress assesses our defense needs and then appropriates the monies to pay for them. The Clinton Administration turned the Constitution on its head, not to mention National Security. Defense Secretary Aspin initiated a so-called "bottom up" review of our military budget after the massive cuts were set in motion. The inevitable result was a political budget document designed to convince people that, despite the cuts, America could still take care of its global responsibilities. This claim was deceitful and bogus.

The U.S. Armed Forces were also being experimented upon by liberal social engineers. Though Clinton's policy of admitting open homosexuals was stopped by Congress, the policy of feminizing the military was implemented with a vengeance. Shortly after taking power, using Tailhook as an excuse, Aspin ignored the findings of the Presidential Commission on the Assignment of Women in the Armed Forces and dramatically expanded the role of women in the military. He did this despite the fact that military women merely on the outskirts of military operations during the Persian Gulf War were taken prisoner by the enemy and raped. Footnote? The Aspin policy guaranteed more sexual abuse — even torture and death of women — during wartime. It also led to well-publicized sexual harassment and abuse incidents.

But perhaps the greatest threat to the U.S. military — illustrated by Michael's case — was the policy of turning control of our forces over to the U.N.

In this context, we cannot forget October 3, 1993 — "Bloody Sunday" for U.S. forces in Somalia. Operating under the overall command and control of the United Nations, an astounding 80 percent of the elite U.S. forces sent to hunt down and capture Somali warlord Mohammed Farah Aidid were either wounded or killed in a fierce battle. Some of the American dead had their bodies stripped naked and their corpses put on grotesque public display, while one American flyer was taken captive and beaten severely by Aidid's forces.

None of this had to happen. They were put in the line of fire by an Administration that had refused to provide them tanks and other armored vehicles. Consequently, our troops were forced to rely for protection on a United Nations military command in Somalia that had already been characterized by chaos and confusion. In fact, one U.N. commander had already been sent home for collaborating with Aidid.

Besides the unnecessary loss of life, the event had another horrible impact: America had been humiliated in front of the entire world because the aftermath was televised. At home, Americans were shocked and saddened. They rendered their verdict in calls to talk shows on radio and television: it was all the fault of foreign policy novice Bill Clinton, elected President of the U.S. even though he had "loathed" the military as a young man and had actively avoided serving his country in the Armed Forces.

Like Pearl Harbor, "Bloody Sunday" in Somalia is a day that will live in infamy. It demonstrated that the great American military fighting machine that had been carefully constructed by the Reagan and Bush Administrations over the course of a decade had been virtually dismantled and demoralized by the Clinton Administration in just a few months.

Equally serious, by subjecting the U.S. military to foreign command and control through the U.N., Clinton has abdicated his own role under the U.S. Constitution as Commander-in-Chief, permitting the U.N. Secretary-General to virtually run U.S. foreign policy. Acting without any Congressional authorization or approval, Clinton has surrendered American sovereignty to a world body.

If this is not an impeachable offense, than what is?

The October 3 incident wasn't as disastrous as the Japanese

attack on Pearl Harbor in terms of casualties, but it was the greatest U.S. military set-back since 241 Marines were killed by a car bomb explosion in Lebanon. The difference was that President Reagan, after the debacle in Lebanon, withdrew our forces and vowed never again to commit our troops to a conflict without the overwhelming force necessary to win it.

President Clinton, on the other hand, expanded our troop presence in Somalia. At the same time, he called off the hunt for warlord Aidid, and held out the prospect of Aidid playing some kind of political role in a future Somalia. Shortly thereafter, some of the U.S. Army Rangers involved in the hunt for Aidid were abruptly sent home. It was a reversal that was truly mind-boggling in its scope. The about-face demonstrated that U.S. foreign policy under Clinton had become a tragic comedy of errors.

Faced with a foreign policy debacle, Clinton and his Defense Secretary, Les Aspin, covered-up and lied about why it happened. Asked why U.S. troops in Somalia were denied the tanks and armored vehicles necessary for their own self-defense, a senior Administration aide said Clinton "picked up the phone and called Les to find out what the hell was going on." This made it appear that Clinton was truly angry about the loss of American life. Clinton later said Aspin told him there had been "no consensus among the Joint Chiefs" to send the armor. This was absolutely false. In fact, the Washington Post reported that Aspin never consulted the chiefs. He had consulted then Joint-Chiefs Chairman General Colin Powell, who had specifically requested the armor.

When the truth finally emerged, Aspin tried to blame President Bush by insisting that the Clinton Administration had "inherited" the Somalia situation. This, too, was a lie. President Bush had always intended to withdraw U.S. forces after the humanitarian mission of feeding the starving was finished. It was Clinton who transformed the mission into "nation building" in Somalia under U.N. control.

In a moving article appearing in USA Today, a grieving father of one of the U.S. Army Rangers killed in that fierce battle in Somalia called for Aspin to go. "Why is Les Aspin our Secretary of Defense?" asked Larry E. Joyce, a retired army lieutenant colonel. "He is too uncaring and too incompetent to command the most precious resource this nation has."

But the real question is, why is Bill Clinton still U.S. President?

Haiti – another Marxist Dictator propped up

It didn't take long for another debacle to occur. As Mr. Clinton was trying to make sense of his own Somalia policy in a nationwide television address, U.S. forces on a U.N. mission to Haiti were stopped from docking in that country when angry citizens turned out to protest the impending return of exiled Haitian President Jean Bertrand Aristide. Once again, American foreign policy was seen as a paper tiger. A few lightly-armed thugs pounding on cars had turned back the American military. Clinton immediately announced the reimposition of economic sanctions on Haiti, designed to force the country's military rulers to accept Aristide's return. Clinton dangled forth the option of sending U.S. troops into Haiti to bring Aristide back to power.

In fact, the Haiti policy was ill-conceived, confused and doomed from the start. During the campaign, Clinton had denounced President Bush for his policy of returning Haitian immigrants back to their country. However, after he was elected, Mr. Clinton quickly realized that the Bush policy was correct, otherwise a flood of Haitian boat people was going to be washing up on American shores. Clinton decided to retain the Bush policy, but proceeded to implement his own scheme to return Aristide to power. After a period of negotiation, Mr. Clinton's aides thought they had made a deal with Haiti's military rulers to return him to power in October.

But the Clinton Administration, in concluding this deal, ignored the available public information showing that Aristide, though democratically-elected, had been forced out because he had unconstitutionally abused the system by grossly violating human rights. Haiti's military — backed by many ordinary Haitians — had demanded that Aristide stand trial for his undemocratic acts as president, among them his endorsement of the use of necklacing against his political opponents, in which a tire is laid around a victim's neck and set on fire. And though Aristide was advertised as a "priest," and therefore someone steeped in Christian compassion, the evidence showed that he was actually kicked out of his religious order for advocating class hatred and violence.

All of this information was available to the Clinton Administration and they decided to back Aristide anyway. That was bad enough. But the policy became even more incomprehensible when word leaked out that the Central Intelligence Agency (CIA) had prepared a profile of Aristide that found him to be a borderline psychopath who took a variety of mind-altering drugs, including lithium.

The lessons were easy to draw. In the Somalia situation, the Clinton Administration had demonstrated its utter contempt for American military commanders and their troops. In the case of Haiti, the Administration ignored the warnings of the intelligence community and used our troops to restore Aristide to power.

Congress failed to challenge this policy. What's more, the media facilitated it. Liberal media figures, such as commentator Bill Moyers, who used to rail against "secret government" in the Reagan years, did not see fit to question Clinton's reliance on the U.N., conducted outside of normal constitutional and budgetary channels, and the transformation of the world body into an organization designed to establish or replace national governments.

The Debt Issue is Fraudulent

This was most apparent in repeated media claims that the U.S. had a financial "debt to the U.N." that had to be paid. Despite these well-publicized claims, no debt actually exists. Claims about a U.S. "debt to the U.N." ignore the billions of dollars' worth of military and other assistance which has been provided to the world organization and which has not been properly credited or reimbursed to the U.S. In effect, the Clinton Administration has been diverting billions of dollars from various federal agencies, especially the Department of Defense, to the U.N. Some of the money came out of military readiness accounts.

This is an impeachable offense. (Remember, impeachment only means that the House finds enough evidence to hold a trial. The Senate tries and either convicts or acquits.)

The drain on funds for military readiness has been obscured by these constant media allegations about a "debt" to the U.N. These allegations have served to distract attention from a Clinton Administration policy of providing resources, personnel and equipment to the U.N. without the approval of Congress. The latest example of this came in April 1998 when it was disclosed that the administration gave the U.N. $200,000 as seed money to mobilize the "standby" U.N. peacekeeping army it has always favored. The administration decided unilaterally to "reprogram" funds that had been appropriated by Congress for another purpose.

Congressman Roscoe Bartlett (R-Md.), a member of the House National Security Committee, believes that such practices have to stop. Thanks to his work, the Congress is now fully aware of the situation and has an opportunity to reassert its constitutional role and authority in this matter. Bartlett has wanted to prevent payment of any "debt" to the U.N. until all US assistance to the U.N. is factored into the U.S./U.N. financial relationship. He also wants the administration to quit the practice of providing "voluntary" assistance worth billions of dollars to the U.N. without advance Congressional approval.

Bartlett points out that a Congressional Research Service (CRS) report finds that the U.S. has paid more than $11 billion on international peacekeeping efforts between 1992 and 1997. Although the report didn't specify how much of this had been counted against U.S. "dues" to the U.N., the figure could be as low as $1.8 billion. This leaves about $9 billion worth of what the administration calls "voluntary" international peacekeeping assistance. But this figure only covers assistance provided by the Department of Defense. Other federal agencies have also been ordered by the administration to support the U.N., bringing the total figure to perhaps $15 billion.

The $1.8 billion figure that was counted against U.S. "dues" to the world body was itself taken from a 1996 General Accounting Office (GAO) report on U.S. costs in support of U.N.-authorized "peace operations" in Haiti, former Yugoslavia, Somalia and Rwanda from fiscal years 1992-1995. The $1.8 billion figure represents the State Department's costs of the operations in question. This is the budget from which the U.S. share of U.N. peacekeeping operations has traditionally been funded. Overall, the GAO found that the costs reported by U.S. government agencies for support of U.N. operations in these areas of the world was over $6.6 billion and that the U.N. had reimbursed the U.S. $79.4 million "for some of these costs." That left about $4.8 billion during this period alone in what the administration called "voluntary" assistance to the world body.

In order to grasp the significance of these figures, the difference between "blue-helmeted" and "green-helmeted" operations has to be fully understood.

The United Nations Participation Act, regulating U.S. involvement with the United Nations, gives the president the limited authority to assign up to 1,000 U.S. military personnel to a Chapter VI U.N. mission only if the U.S. government can show it is not a Chapter VII operation, which requires Congressional approval.[12] Chapter VI missions are non-combatant in nature. As noted, Department of Defense figures from March 1997 claimed there were only 522 U.S. personnel deployed under the auspices of the U.N. Participation Act or the U.S. Foreign Assistance Act. Under these circumstances, involving U.N. "operational control" of the troops, the Pentagon says "the UN is paying the bill" because they are considered blue-helmeted. As of March 1997, 489 personnel were assigned to the so-called U.N. Preventive Deployment in Macedonia, which, as Senator Mitch McConnell has noted, lacks "a clear, legal mandate" because the Administration falsely claimed it was a Chapter VI mission that did not require Congressional approval.

In any case, a far greater number of "green helmet" U.S. military personnel who volunteered for the U.S. military are in fact deployed on behalf of the U.N. These are personnel who do not wear U.N. helmets or carry U.N. identify cards. They do not report to foreign U.N. commanders. And their costs are being paid by the Department of Defense — that is, U.S. taxpayers.

Those March 27, 1997 Pentagon figures asserted there were 68,790 U.S. forces serving the U.N. or involved in peace-keeping activities. The figures were on a document labeled, "US Forces Participating in, or Acting in Support of Selected UN Operations, UNSC [U.N. Security Council] Resolutions, or Non-U.N. Peacekeeping Activities." This figure include U.S. personnel in Macedonia (said to be 511 in this document) as well as 1,052 personnel involved in "non-UN Peace Operations" in the Middle East and Latin America. It also includes 67,200 "supporting enforcement" of U.N. Security Council resolutions in Bosnia, Iraq, and Korea.

---

[12] United States Code Annotated, Title 22, Foreign Relations and Intercourse, Section 287d. Use of armed forces; limitations; Section 287-d1, non-combatant assistance to United Nations.

In other words, according to the Pentagon itself, there were about 68,000 U.S. troops serving the U.N. However, they were deployed on behalf of the U.N. without the explicit approval of the U.S. Congress. And what's worse, the bill goes not to the U.N. but to the Congress for payment.

It is clearly not the intention of Rep. Bartlett and his supporters to have the U.N. pick up the tab for all of these operations. For example, the Congress could decide that it is entirely proper for it to fund the deployment of some 37,000 troops in Korea, even though they are technically there under U.N. authority. It may also be the case that the Congress would want to fund the Bosnia deployment, although it is technically being conducted under the auspices of both the U.N. and NATO. What Bartlett and his colleagues are arguing for is a full accounting and no "debt" payments until the U.S. is given credit or reimbursement for what is truly in our national interest. This is a decision, Bartlett argues, that quite properly and constitutionally belongs with Congress.

Where is Congress on Michael New?

It should be noted that Rep. Bartlett, a true leader in Congress on national security issues, also took the lead in trying to clear Michael's name. Along with Rep. Helen Chenoweth, of Idaho, he introduced a House Resolution which condemned the court-martial of Michael and called on the president to vindicate him, override his conviction, and restore him to a place of honor in the Army. In another legislative effort that grew out of Michael's case, Rep. Tom DeLay (R-Texas), the House Majority Whip, introduced a bill in 1995 that would have prohibited the President from forcing American troops to wear UN uniforms. In the Senate, a similar bill was introduced by Senators Bob Dole and Larry Craig. However, Dole, who became the Republican presidential nominee in 1996, failed to express direct support for Michael's cause.

At a news conference announcing support for this legislation in the House, Rep. DeLay declared, "A soldier's oath is to the U.S. Constitution, not to the UN Charter. Forcing soldiers to wear the uniform of the United Nations effectively asks the soldier to serve another power. No American soldier should be put in Michael New's position — forced to choose allegiances between the United States and the United Nations." DeLay said about New, "He is willing to fight and die for his country, but he is not willing to fight and die for the United Nations. Frankly, I can't blame him."

We greatly appreciate the efforts of Reps. Helen Chenoweth, Tom DeLay, Roscoe Bartlett, Bob Barr, Jim Traficant, Sonny Bono, and scores of other members of Congress. In fact, on September 5, 1996, the House voted 277-129 to pass Bartlett's bill, H.R. 3308, which would have prohibited members of our Armed Forces from being forced to wear the U.N. uniform and insignia. So no one can say that there has not been Congressional support.

The Senate, on the other hand, has been very quiet on this subject.

Phil Gramm, of Texas, has given some great speeches on the topic, getting standing ovations when he was running for president by pounding the podium and shouting, "If I am elected president, your sons and daughters will never have to serve under a United Nations Army!" In September 1995, he gave that speech to The Conservative Women for America in Washington, D.C., not knowing that one of his constituents, Michael New, was sitting in the audience listening. After the speech, Colonel Ray and Michael stopped the senator in the hall where Michael shook his hand and said, "Great speech, Senator. That's just what they're trying to do to me. I'm from Texas. You're my senator. Will you help me?" Gramm looked very surprised, murmured, "My staff is working on it," and scooted for his limousine. Gramm's staff has been courteous, but has not been forthcoming with any help, despite repeated requests verbally and in writing. In general, it's been difficult to get to a decision-maker. We've met something of a stone wall trying to get past the receptionist. Calls were not returned, and we finally gave up, deciding that a man running for president is too busy to deal with the needs of one constituent, regardless of how important we thought the issue was for our nation. We can understand that.

On the radio and in meeting halls around the country, I have been asked about where Senator Phil Gramm stands on helping Michael New. These are generally conservative audiences, and I don't doubt that the Senator has had supporters among my listeners. I have simply related the story of what happened. I have tried to leave open a door for Gramm to come on board, but I'm not going to lie for the man.

Imagine our surprise when we recently asked our friends to call their congressmen for legislative support to hear that one who called Senator Gramm's office was told, "Why should Senator Gramm help Michael New when his father has been criticizing [Gramm] on the radio?" Imagine that! They're not deaf, after all! But apparently Senator Gramm is more concerned with his image than with the sovereignty of his nation or with the plight of an individual Texan. We welcome the Senator to join our cause at any point, but we will continue to tell the truth about his actions.

We must express our appreciation to Senator Mitch McConnell, of Kentucky, who finally listened to Colonel Ray, his constituent, and agreed to come on board. He made a commitment and stood by it. How refreshing.

The bottom line is that Congress as a whole has failed to act to protect Michael and all our armed forces, and it did not successfully challenge Clinton's pro-U.N. policy. At this point, besides our continuing legal appeals and educational efforts, the option of impeachment seems to remain a viable option.

What is "Civilian Control?"

The failure of Army Chief of Staff, Dennis Reimer, to take action on Michael's behalf, was disappointing but telling. Reimer was fully informed of the facts in the Michael New case. In a letter to Reimer, Reps. Bartlett and DeLay, along with more than 60 members of Congress informed Reimer that the bill to prohibit the wearing of the U.N. uniform would not have been necessary had the U.S. Army followed its own regulations "and properly understood the Constitution and U.S. statutes enacted by Congress."[13]

Some might say, of course, that Reimer had no choice, based on the position taken by his boss, President Clinton.

Duane Thorin, POW in Korea, and recognized authority on military/civilian issues in the Fifties and Sixties, disagrees with the above position, pointing out that "civilian control" does not mean that the President is in control of the military. When there is a declared war, he is the Commander in Chief. That is a military position. "Civilian control" means Congressional control. Thorin points out that this was the original concept, but that in recent years schools have begun to teach just the opposite.

This is a key point, and is at the heart of the current struggle between the executive branch and the legislative branch of our federal government. For several years now, Congress has seemed uninterested in jealously guarding its prerogatives and its power as delineated in the Constitution, and as anticipated by the Founding Fathers. For many congressmen, it appears that getting re-elected is the only concern they have.

Even U. S. District Judge Paul Friedman, who denied Michael New's first writ of habeas corpus, touched on this issue by stating that Michael has "...raised serious Constitutional questions which have never been answered about the relationship between the Executive Branch and the Legislative Branch."

---

[13] Reps. Roscoe Bartlett and Tom DeLay, Letter to General Dennis Reimer, December 6, 1995.

Colonel Ron Ray's point bears repeating – that the treatment of Michael is an indication of how "compromised" the Army has become. It reflects, he says, "the degree to which our military is willing to accommodate political pressures which do not stand constitutional or legal scrutiny."

Unfortunately, even some conservatives initially failed to support Michael. Patrick J. Buchanan, who emerged as a leading Republican contender with Senator Dole for the presidential nomination, at first balked at supporting Michael. He called it a case of obeying the "legitimate orders of his commander." Buchanan said that Michael "should not disobey orders and as one who aspires to be commander-in chief, I don't think you can tell an American soldier to disobey orders."[14] It speaks well of Patrick Buchanan that, after carefully researching the case, he changed his position, and declared unequivocal support for Michael New, hailing his courage and bravery. Support for Michael became a common theme in his presidential campaign speeches and he vowed, if elected president, to pardon Michael.

Alan Keyes, on the other hand, leapt to the same quick conclusion, even telling Michael Farris to his face that, "If I were President, Michael New would go to prison." But when offered evidence to support Michael's stand, Keyes steadfastly refused to look at it. To this day he claims to be opposed to U.N. dominance, while arguing that Michael, "should have gone through proper channels." We contend that Michael did go through proper channels, alerting his chain of command, filling out endless paperwork, discussing the issue with chaplains, attorneys, sergeants and officers, at great length. This is not something he just woke up and did without giving the Army due notice.

Howard Phillips, chairman of Conservative Caucus and presidential candidate of the U.S. Taxpayers Party in 1996, has been an early and consistent supporter of Michael and our

---

[14] Buchanan appearance on the CNN Evans & Novak program, October 7, 1995.

cause. He has also been one of the leading proponents of a congressional impeachment inquiry into President Clinton's conduct and policies. Phillips has exhibited true moral courage, giving up a comfortable career in Washington under Republican leadership, because they consistently speak out against the New World Order, but consistently vote for more of it.

When Michael came to the States in September of 1995, for a conference with attorneys and a chance to meet the growing number of supporters, Phillips arranged for an interview with several leading columnists and journalists, including Charley Reese, Joseph Sobran, and Samuel Francis. Phillips' support has been unwavering.

Duty, Honor, Country

In his famous speech at the U.S. Military Academy at West Point in 1962, General Douglas MacArthur said that three hallowed words — duty, honor, country – "reverently dictate what you want to be, what you can be, and what you will be." He explained, "They are your rallying point to build courage when courage seems to fail, to regain faith when there seems to be little cause for faith, to create hope when hope becomes forlorn." General MacArthur told those cadets,

"Yours is the profession of arms, the will to win, the sure knowledge that in war there is no substitute for victory, that if you lose, the nation will be destroyed, that the very obsession of your public service must be duty, honor, country."

U.S. Army Field Manual 22-100, "Military Leadership," is given to every recruit in Boot Camp. Every soldier is told, in writing:

"Moral courage is as important as physical courage. It is the courage to stand firm on your values, your moral principles, and your convictions. You show moral courage when you do something based on one of your values or moral principles, knowing that the action may not be in your best interest.

"It takes special courage to support unpopular decisions and to make it difficult for others to do the wrong thing. Others may encourage you to 'embrace a slightly' unethical solution as the easiest or most convenient method. Do not ease the way for others to do wrong; stand up for your beliefs and what you know is right. Do not compromise your professional ethic or your individual values and moral principles. If you believe you are right after sober and considered judgment, hold your position."[15]

Specialist Michael New was doing what he was trained to do. We believe Michael showed moral courage in the tradition of many who have sacrificed careers and comfort in order to stand for principle.

It is incumbent upon us that we follow those who set such courageous examples. We call on our veterans, active duty military personnel, indeed all American people to take a stand – now.

The fate of our nation literally hangs in the balance. Will we be a Republic in twenty years? Or will we be a vassal state under the New Lords of the Earth?

One of our favorite historical figures, Scottish patriot William Wallace of "Braveheart" fame, said it well when he sensed that his countrymen had lost heart. He asked, "What will you do without freedom?" Duty, honor and country are calling us.

When Michael joined the Army, we knew that he was entering into a "dark place." Having recently rededicated his life to Christ, we felt that an Army barracks is a poor place for a young Christian to grow, spiritually. This is why Suzanne and I prayed virtually every single day for over two years that he would, "be a bright light in a dark place." We had no idea how God would answer that prayer, but we will always believe that

---

[15] Field Manual 22-100, Leadership. U.S. Army. (Get details) Currently being re-written, presumably to eliminate this little section, or at least to redefine it to protect themselves from future men with leadership potential who might have the temerity to actually do what they are trained to do.

it was Him at work in Michael New that gave Mike such a clarity of understanding on the issues before him, and the implications in such an order.

The bottom line is that "no man can serve two masters." This is as true in the political and legal realms as it is in the spiritual realm. Michael New understood it. The question now to be determined is whether the leaders of this country can be brought to understand it. If they cannot, then this Republic will not only die, but deserves to do so.

May God bless America, once again.

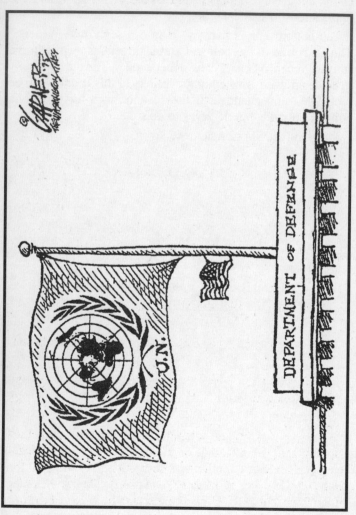

Used by permission.

Appendices

CITE: 10 USC Sec. 502   01/03/95
          EXPCITE: TITLE 10 - ARMED FORCES
              Subtitle A - General Military Law

PART II - PERSONNEL
CHAPTER 31 - ENLISTMENTS

HEAD   Sec. 502. Enlistment oath: who may administer

STATUTE   Each person enlisting in an armed force shall take the following oath:

''I, _ _ _ _ _ _ _ _ _, do solemnly swear (or affirm) that I will support and defend the Constitution of the United States against all enemies, foreign and domestic; that I will bear true faith and allegiance to the same; and that I will obey the orders of the President of the United States and the orders of the officers appointed over me, according to regulations and the Uniform Code of Military Justice.

So help me God!"

This oath may be taken before any commissioned officer of any armed force.

United Nations Oath

The oath which commanding officers of UN deployments take:

"I solemnly affirm to exercise in all loyalty, discretion and conscience the functions entrusted to me as a member of the international service of the United Nations, to discharge those functions and regulate my conduct with the interest of the United Nations only in view, and not to seek or accept instructions in respect to the performance of my duties from any government or other authority external to the organization."

It is our understanding that the above oath was taken by Finland's General Engstrom, commanding officer over Michael New's battalion which served in Macedonia.

LETTER FROM SPC. MICHAEL NEW TO HIS CHAIN OF COMMAND, EXPLAINING HIS STAND AND REQUESTING FURTHER DIRECTION.

18 September 1995

FROM:	Spc Michael G. New
	HHC 1/15th Infantry
	Conn Barracks
	Schweinfurt, Germany
TO:	Chain of Command
Subject:	Statement of Spc. New concerning wearing U.N. uniform.

Reference (a) Oral orders of 21 August 1995 to submit statement following research.

1. Pursuant to Ref. (a) in compliance with orders received on or about 21 August 1995, I researched the U.N. Charter, history and objectives of the U.N., and submit enclosures (1), my statement requested of me by my CO of my convictions and position regarding wearing a U.N. uniform and serving under U.N. command. Enclosure (1) attached hereto is submitted in specific compliance with those orders.

2. I have reviewed the U.N. Charter, its history and objectives which I was somewhat familiar with, and I still find that the U.S. Constitution and Declaration of Independence are incompatible with the U.N. Charter. My statement is submitted, and I await further direction.

Spc Michael G. New, U.S.A.

1. As an American soldier I fully intend to obey all lawful orders, and I again request that the Army through
   appropriate channels provide for my review the legal
   justification for the change of uniform and the justification for pending deployment orders for UN/NATO
   operation "Prevent Deployment – Able Sentry".
   Please include any and all relevant acts of the U.S.
   Congress and/or U.N. Security Council Resolutions.

2. On August 21, 1995, my seniors in the U.S. Army
   chain of command informed me that my unit and I
   would soon be ordered to significantly alter our uniform by sewing a United Nations patch on my right
   shoulder and wearing the blue beret and/or helmet of
   the U.N. These are important insignia. If they were
   unimportant, then I would not have been threatened
   with courts-martial, imprisonment, or less than dishonorable discharge when I expressed my reserva-
   tions about wearing them. I interpret the wearing of
   a uniform, or the accoutrements of a uniform, as a
   sign of allegiance and faithfulness to the authority or
   power so signified, or which issues that uniform. I
   am an American citizen who was recruited for and
   voluntarily joined the U.S. Army to serve as an
   American soldier. I am not a citizen of the United
   Nations. I am not a United Nations Fighting Person.
   I have never taken an oath to the United Nations, but
   I have taken the required oath to support and defend
   the Constitution of the United States.

3. I am not trying to avoid a difficult or dangerous
   assignment or to get out of the Army. I served in
   Kuwait last year and have offered to serve anywhere
   in the world, in my American uniform, in my capacity as a U.S. Army medic under American command
   and U.S. Constitutional protections. I have worked

diligently to be a good soldier. I have previously been offered a "Green to Gold" program to an Army Commission, and I am still seriously considering that offer. In order to avoid controversy, or to avoid placing the Army in a bad light, I have requested a transfer to a unit that is not required to wear the U.N. uniform. I was told that such is not possible, and I was even reluctantly willing to accept an honorable discharge, and I was willing to sadly and reluctantly withdraw from the U.S. Army quietly. However, I will not wear a U.N. uniform or serve under U.N. command, and I will strongly contest any discharge that is less than honorable.

4. I simply cannot understand the legal basis of the Army order to change my uniform against my oath of enlistment, against my conscience and against my will. Despite my requests for information up my chain of command, my questions about the lawfulness of such an order or about how my allegiance can be transferred without my approval have gone unanswered.

5. My parents share my deep concerns and have requested information and help from General Dennis Reimer, Army Chief of Staff in Washington, D.C., in getting answers to my questions and theirs. To date, we have received no answer or information.

6. My chain of command has directed me to study the history and objectives of the U.N. My knowledge of, and my research into the United Nations, (which continues even as I prepare this statement), indicates to me that the U.N. Charter is based upon man-made principles which are incompatible with the Constitution of the United States, and the U.N.'s authority and principles are diametrically opposed to

the founding documents of my country. The more I study U.N. history and American history, the more incompatible they appear to me.

My studies indicate to me that there are those who would see my country assimilated or brought under the authority of the United Nations, which I interpret to mean a corresponding loss of sovereignty, which is a departure from our Founding Principles and a loss of independence for all Americans. Boutros-Ghali, for example, has written, "The time of absolute and exclusive sovereignty has passed." (1992, An Agenda for Peace) I should expect EVERY American soldier to be concerned about serving under such a Secretary General.

7. I took an oath to defend the Constitution of the United States of America against all enemies, foreign and domestic. I believe that the Constitution is the fundamental law of America, and if there is any ambiguity or conflict with treaty or international agreement or organization that the U.S. Constitution would prevail. My oath is to the Constitution. I cannot find any reference to the United Nations in that oath. That oath includes a statement that is more than a passing reference to God Almighty, it is a prayer, "...so help me God." It is no secret that our nation is founded upon Biblical principles. {*} Our Founders reflected this fact in their speeches, correspondence and documents from the Mayflower Compact to the Declaration of Independence, and other more recent documents, all of which recognize certain rights such as life, liberty and property as being bestowed from Above, and as, therefore, "unalienable." I believe I will lose something precious and more valuable than the U.N. can possibly grant me, by surrendering my

status as an American fighting man.

8. Without a response from the Army about the legality of any orders to become a U.N. soldier, I do not intend to surrender my status as an American soldier to wear the uniform of a foreign power. If you wish to convene a courts-martial and send me to jail for standing upon my oath as an American soldier and for defending my wearing the American Army uniform, and its historic significance, then I cannot prevent that action, and I will accept it as a price I am willing to pay, rather than submit to an order to obey or render allegiance to any foreign power, including the United Nations.

(signed) Spc. Michael G. New

* "Our law and our institutions must necessarily be based upon and embody the teachings of the Redeemer of mankind. It is impossible that it should be otherwise; and in this sense and to this extent our civilization and our institutions are emphatically Christian. ...[T]his is a religious people. This is historically true. From the discovery of this continent to the present hour, there is a single voice making this affirmation...we find everywhere a clear recognition of the same truth...this is a Christian nation."

— Justice David J. Brewer
Holy Trinity Church v. U.S.

PRESIDENTIAL DECISION DIRECTIVE 25

Unlawful Deployment

Clinton Administration Policy on Reforming Multilateral Peace Operations (PDD 25) Released on the WWW by the Bureau of International Organizational Affairs, U.S. Department of State, February 22, 1996

The document below was: "Released on the WWW by the Bureau of International Organizational Affairs, U.S. Department of State, February 22, 1996." This State Department release is an unclassified summary. The details of the actual Secret PDD 25 are still concealed from public scrutiny.

EXECUTIVE SUMMARY

Last year, President Clinton ordered an inter-agency review of our nation's peacekeeping policies and programs in order to develop a comprehensive policy framework suited to the realities of the post-Cold War period. This policy review has resulted in a Presidential Decision Directive (PDD 25). The President signed this directive, following the completion of extensive consultations with Members of Congress. This paper summarizes the key elements of that directive.

As specified in the Bottom-Up Review, the primary mission of the U.S. Armed Forces remains to be prepared to fight and win two simultaneous regional conflicts. In this context, peacekeeping can be one useful tool to help prevent and resolve such conflicts before they pose direct threats to our national security. Peacekeeping can also serve U.S. interests by promoting democracy, regional security, and economic growth.

The policy directive (PDD) addresses six major issues of reform and improvement: **Making disciplined and coherent choices about which peace operations to support** — both when we vote in the Security Council for UN peace operations and when we participate in such operations with U.S. troops. To achieve this goal, the policy directive sets forth three increasingly rigorous standards of review for U.S. support for or participation in peace operations, with the most stringent applying to U.S. participation in missions that may involve combat. The policy directive affirms that peacekeeping can be a useful tool for advancing U.S. national security interests in some circumstances, but both U.S. and UN involvement in peacekeeping must be selective and more effective.

Reducing U.S. costs for UN peace operations, both the percentage our nation pays for each operation and the cost of the operations themselves. To achieve this goal, the policy directive orders that we work to reduce our peacekeeping assessment percentage from the current 31.7% to 25% by January 1, 1996, and proposes a number of specific steps to reduce the cost of UN peace operations.

Defining clearly our policy regarding the command and control of American military forces in UN peace operations. The policy directive underscores the fact that the President will never relinquish command of U.S. forces. However, as Commander-in-Chief, the President has the authority to place U.S. forces under the operational control of a foreign commander when doing so serves American security interests, just as American leaders have done numerous times since the Revolutionary War, including in Operation Desert Storm. The greater the anticipated U.S. military role, the less likely it will be that the U.S. will agree to have a UN commander exercise overall operational control over U.S. forces. Any large scale participation of U.S. forces in a major peace enforcement operation that is likely to involve combat should ordinarily be conducted under U.S. command and operational control or through competent regional organizations such as NATO or ad hoc coalitions.

Reforming and improving the UN's capability to manage peace operations. The policy recommends 11 steps to strengthen UN management of peace operations and directs U.S. support for strengthening the UN's planning, logistics, information and command and control capabilities.

Improving the way the U.S. government manages and funds peace operations. The policy directive creates a new "shared responsibility" approach to managing and funding UN peace operations within the U.S. Government. Under this approach, the Department of Defense will take lead management and funding responsibility for those UN operations that involve U.S. combat units and those that are likely to involve combat, whether or not U.S. troops are involved. This approach will ensure that military expertise is brought to bear on those operations that have a significant military component. The State Department will retain lead management and funding responsibility for traditional peacekeeping operations that do not involve U.S. combat units. In all cases, the State Department remains responsible for the conduct of diplomacy and instructions to embassies and our UN Mission in New York.

Creating better forms of cooperation between the Executive, the Congress and the American public on peace operations. The policy directive sets out seven proposals for increasing and regularizing the flow of information and consultation between the executive branch and Congress; the President believes U.S. support for and participation in UN peace operations can only succeed over the long term with the bipartisan support of Congress and the American people.

KEY ELEMENTS OF THE CLINTON ADMINISTRATION'S POLICY ON REFORMING

MULTILATERAL PEACE OPERATIONS (AS SPECIFIED IN PDD 25, MAY 1994)

Introduction: The Role of Peace Operations in U.S. Foreign Policy

Serious threats to the security of the United States still exist in the post-Cold War era. New threats will emerge. The United States remains committed to meeting such threats. When our interests dictate, the U.S. must be willing and able to fight and win wars, unilaterally whenever necessary. To do so, we must create the required capabilities and maintain them ready to use. UN peace operations cannot substitute for this requirement. (Note: For simplicity, the term peace operations is used in this document to cover the entire spectrum of activities from traditional peacekeeping to peace enforcement aimed at defusing and resolving international conflicts.) Circumstances will arise, however, when multilateral action best serves U.S. interests in preserving or restoring peace. In such cases, the UN can be an important instrument for collective action. UN peace operations can also provide a "force multiplier" in our efforts to promote peace and stability.

During the Cold War, the United Nations could resort to multilateral peace operations only in the few cases when the interests of the Soviet Union and the West did not conflict. In the new strategic environment such operations can serve more often as a cost-effective tool to advance American as well as collective interests in maintaining peace in key regions and create global burden-sharing for peace.

Territorial disputes, armed ethnic conflicts, civil wars (many of which could spill across international borders) and the collapse of governmental authority in some states are among the current threats to peace. While many of these conflicts may not directly threaten American interests, their cumulative effect is significant.

The UN has sought to play a constructive role in such situations by mediating disputes and obtaining agreement to cease-fires and political settlements. Where such agreements have been reached, the interposition of neutral forces under UN auspices has, in many cases, helped facilitate lasting peace. UN peace operations have served important U.S. national interests. In Cambodia, UN efforts led to an election protected by peacekeepers, the return of hundreds of thousands of refugees and the end of a destabilizing regional conflict. In El Salvador, the UN sponsored elections and is helping to end a long and bitter civil war. The UN's supervision of Namibia's transition to independence removed a potential source of conflict in strategic southern Africa and promoted democracy.

The UN in Cyprus has prevented the outbreak of war between two NATO allies. Peacekeeping on the Golan Heights has helped preserve peace between Israel and Syria. In Former Yugoslavia, the UN has provided badly-needed humanitarian assistance and helped prevent the conflict from spreading to other parts of the region. UN-imposed sanctions against Iraq, coupled with the peacekeeping operation on the Kuwait border, are constraining Iraq's ability to threaten its neighbors.

Need for Reform

While serving U.S. interests, UN peace operations continue to require improvement and reform. Currently, each operation is created and managed separately, and economies of scale are lost. Likewise, further organizational changes at UN Headquarters would improve efficiency and effectiveness. A fully independent office of Inspector General should be established immediately. The U.S. assessment rate should be reduced to 25 per cent. Since it is in our interest at times to support UN peace operations, it is also in our interest to seek to strengthen UN peacekeeping capabilities and to make operations less expensive and peacekeeping management more accountable. Similarly, it is in our interest to identify clearly and quickly those peace operations we will support and those we will not. Our policy establishes clear guidelines for making such decisions.

Role in U.S. Foreign Policy: UN and other multilateral peace operations will at times offer the best way to prevent, contain or resolve conflicts that could otherwise be more costly and deadly. In such cases, the U.S. benefits from having to bear only a share of the burden. We also benefit by being able to invoke the voice of the community of nations on behalf of a cause we support. Thus, establishment of a capability to conduct multilateral peace operations is part of our National Security Strategy and National Military Strategy.

While the President never relinquishes command of U.S. forces, the participation of U.S. military personnel in UN operations can, in particular circumstances, serve U.S. interests.

First, U.S. military participation may, at times, be necessary to persuade others to participate in operations that serve U.S. interests.

Second, U.S. participation may be one way to exercise U.S. influence over an important UN mission, without unilaterally bearing the burden.

Third, the U.S. may be called upon and choose to provide unique capabilities to important operations that other countries cannot.

In improving our capabilities for peace operations, we will not discard or weaken other tools for achieving U.S. objectives. If U.S. participation in a peace operation were to interfere with our basic military strategy, winning two major regional conflicts nearly simultaneously (as established in the Bottom Up Review), we would place our national interest uppermost. The U.S. will maintain the capability to act unilaterally or in coalitions when our most significant interests and those of our friends and allies are at stake. Multilateral peace operations must, therefore, be placed in proper perspective among the instruments of U.S. foreign policy.

The U.S. does not support a standing UN army, nor will we earmark specific U.S. military units for participation in UN operations. We will provide information about U.S. capabilities for data bases and planning purposes.

It is not U.S. policy to seek to expand either the number of UN peace operations or U.S. involvement in such operations. Instead, this policy, which builds upon work begun by previous administrations and is informed by the concerns of the Congress and our experience in recent peace operations, aims to ensure that our use of peacekeeping is selective and more effective. Congress must also be actively involved in the continuing implementation of U.S. policy on peacekeeping.

I. Supporting the Right Peace Operations
i. Voting for Peace Operations

The U.S. will support well-defined peace operations, generally, as a tool to provide finite windows of opportunity to allow combatants to resolve their differences and failed societies to begin to reconstitute themselves. Peace operations should not be open-ended commitments but instead linked to concrete political solutions; otherwise, they normally should not be undertaken. To the greatest extent possible, each UN peace operation should have a specified timeframe tied to intermediate or final objectives, an integrated political/military strategy well-coordinated with humanitarian assistance efforts, specified troop levels, and a firm budget estimate. The U.S. will continue to urge the UN Secretariat and Security Council members to engage in rigorous, standard evaluations of all proposed new peace operations. The Administration will consider the factors below when deciding whether to vote for a proposed new UN peace operation (Chapter VI or Chapter VII) or to support a regionally-sponsored peace operation:

— UN involvement advances U.S. interests, and there

is an international community of interest for dealing with the problem on a multilateral basis.

There is a threat to or breach of international peace and security, often of a regional character, defined as one or a combination of the following:

International aggression, or;

Urgent humanitarian disaster coupled with violence;

Sudden interruption of established democracy or gross violation of human rights coupled with violence, or threat of violence.

— There are clear objectives and an understanding of where the mission fits on the spectrum between traditional peacekeeping and peace enforcement.

— For traditional (Chapter VI) peacekeeping operations, a ceasefire should be in place and the consent of the parties obtained before the force is deployed.

— For peace enforcement (Chapter VII) operations, the threat to international peace and security is considered significant.

— The means to accomplish the mission are available, including the forces, financing and mandate appropriate to the mission.

— The political, economic and humanitarian consequences of inaction by the international community have been weighed and are considered unacceptable.

— The operation's anticipated duration is tied to clear objectives and realistic criteria for ending the operation.

These factors are an aid in decision-making; they do not by themselves constitute a prescriptive device. Decisions have been and will be based on the cumulative weight of the factors, with no single factor necessarily being an absolute determinant.

In addition, using the factors above, the U.S. will continue to scrutinize closely all existing peace operations when they come up for regular renewal by the Security Council to assess the value of continuing them. In appropriate cases, the U.S. will seek voluntary contributions by beneficiary nations or enhanced host nation support to reduce or cover, at least partially, the costs of certain UN operations. The U.S. will also consider voting against renewal of certain long-standing peace operations that are failing to meet established objectives in order to free military and financial resources for more pressing UN missions.

ii. Participating in UN and Other Peace Operations

The Administration will continue to apply even stricter standards when it assesses whether to recommend to the President that U.S. personnel participate in a given peace operation. In addition to the factors listed above, we will consider the following factors:

— Participation advances U.S. interests and both the unique and general risks to American personnel have been weighed and are considered acceptable.

— Personnel, funds and other resources are available;

— U.S. participation is necessary for operation's success;

— The role of U.S. forces is tied to clear objectives and an endpoint for U.S. participation can be identified;

— Domestic and Congressional support exists or can be marshaled;

— Command and control arrangements are acceptable. Additional, even more rigorous factors will be applied when there is the possibility of significant U.S. participation in Chapter VII operations that are likely to involve combat:

— There exists a determination to commit sufficient forces to achieve clearly defined objectives;

— There exists a plan to achieve those objectives decisively;

— There exists a commitment to reassess and adjust, as necessary, the size, composition, and disposition of our forces to achieve our objectives.

Any recommendation to the President will be based on the cumulative weight of the above factors, with no single factor necessarily being an absolute determinant.

II. The Role of Regional Organizations

In some cases, the appropriate way to perform peace operations will be to involve regional organizations. The U.S. will continue to emphasize the UN as the primary international body with the authority to conduct peacekeeping operations. At the same time, the U.S. will support efforts to improve regional organizations' peacekeeping capabilities. When regional organizations or groupings seek to conduct peacekeeping with UNSC endorsement, U.S. support will be conditioned on adherence to the principles of the UN Charter and meeting established UNSC criteria, including neutrality, consent of the conflicting parties, formal UNSC oversight and finite, renewal mandates.

With respect to the question of peacekeeping in the territory of the former Soviet Union, requests for traditional UN blue-helmeted operations will be considered on the same basis as other requests, using the factors previously outlined (e.g., a threat to international peace and security, clear objectives, etc.). U.S. support for these operations will, as with other such requests, be conditioned on adherence to the principles of the UN Charter and established UNSC criteria.

III. Reducing Costs

Although peacekeeping can be a good investment for the

U.S., it would be better and more sustainable if it cost less. The Administration is committed to reducing the U.S. share of peacekeeping costs to 25% by January 1, 1996, down from the current rate of 31.7%.

We will also inform the UN of Congress' likely refusal to fund U.S. peacekeeping assessments at a rate higher than 25% after Fiscal Year 1995. The Administration remains concerned that the UN has not rectified management inefficiencies that result in excessive costs and, on occasion, fraud and abuse. As a matter of priority, the U.S. will continue to press for dramatic administrative and management improvements in the UN system. In particular, the U.S. is working hard to ensure that new and on-going peace operations are cost-effective and properly managed. Towards this end, the U.S. is pursuing a number of finance and budget management reforms, including:

— immediate establishment of a permanent, fully independent office of Inspector General with oversight responsibility that includes peacekeeping;

— unified budget for all peace operations, with a contingency fund, financed by a single annual peacekeeping assessment;

— standing cadre of professional budget experts from member states, particularly top contributing countries, to assist the UN in developing credible budgets and financial plans;

— enlargement of the revolving peacekeeping reserve fund to $500 million, using voluntary contributions;

— Required status of forces/mission agreements that provide preferential host nation support to peacekeeping operations;

— prohibit UN borrowing from peacekeeping funds to finance cash shortfalls in regular UN administrative operations;

— revise the special peacekeeping scale of assessments to base it on a 3-year average of national income and rationalize Group C so that higher income countries pay their regular budget rate.

Moreover, the U.S. will use its voice and vote in the Fifth Committee of the General Assembly of the United Nations to contain costs of UN peace operations once they are underway.

IV. Strengthening the UN

If peace operations are to be effective and efficient when the U.S. believes they are necessary, the UN must improve the way peace operations are managed. Our goal is not to create a global high command but to enable the UN to manage its existing load more effectively. At present each UN operation is created and managed separately by a still somewhat under-staffed UN Department of Peacekeeping Operations (DPKO). As a result, support to the field may suffer, economies of scale are lost, and work is duplicated. Moreover, the UN's command and control capabilities, particularly in complex operations, need substantial improvement. Structural changes at UN Headquarters, some of which are already underway, would make a positive difference.

The U.S. proposals include the reconfiguration and expansion of the staff for the Department of Peacekeeping Operations to create:

— Plans Division to conduct adequate advance planning and preparation for new and on-going operation;

— Information and Research Division linked to field operations to obtain and provide current information, manage a 24 hour watch center, and monitor open source material and non-sensitive information submitted by governments;

— Operations Division with a modern command, control and communications(C3) architecture based on commercial systems;

— Logistics Division to manage both competitive commercial contracts (which should be re-bid regularly on the basis of price and performance) and a cost-effective logistics computer network to link the UN DPKO with logistics offices in participating member nations. This system would enable the UN to request price and availability data and to order materiel from participating states;

— Small Public Affairs cell dedicated to supporting ongoing peace operations and disseminating information within host countries in order to reduce the risks to UN personnel and increase the potential for mission success;

— Small Civilian Police Cell to manage police missions, plan for the establishment of police and judicial institutions, and develop standard procedures, doctrine and training.

B. To eliminate lengthy, potentially disastrous delays after a mission has been authorized, the UN should establish:

— a rapidly deployable headquarters team, a composite initial logistics support unit, and open, pre-negotiated commercial contracts for logistics support in new mission;

— data base of specific, potentially available forces or capabilities that nations could provide for the full range of peacekeeping and humanitarian operations;

— trained civilian reserve corps to serve as a ready, external talent pool to assist in the administration, management, and execution of UN peace operations;

— modest airlift capability available through pre-negotiated contracts with commercial firms or member states to support urgent deployments.

C. Finally, the UN should establish a professional Peace Operations Training Program for commanders and other military and civilian personnel.

D. Consistent with the specific proposals outlined above, the U.S. will actively support efforts in the Fifth Committee of the General Assembly to redeploy resources within the UN to enable the effective augmentation of the UN DPKO along the lines outlined above. In addition, the U.S. is prepared to undertake the following, primarily on a reimbursable basis:

— detail appropriate numbers of civilian and military personnel to DPKO in New York in advisory or support roles;

— share information, as appropriate, while ensuring full protection of sources and methods;

— offer to design a command, control, and communications systems architecture for the Operations Division, using commercially available systems and software;

— offer to assist DPKO to establish an improved, cost-effective logistics system to support UN peacekeeping operations;

— offer to help design the database of military forces or capabilities and to notify DPKO to establish an improved, cost-effective logistics system to support UN peacekeeping operations;

— offer to help design the database of military forces or capabilities and to notify DPKO, for inclusion in the database, of specific U.S. capabilities that could be made available for the full spectrum of peacekeeping or humanitarian operations. U.S. notification in no way implies a commitment to provide those capabilities, if asked by the UN;

— detail public affairs specialists to the UN;

— offer to help create and establish a training program, participate in peacekeeping training efforts and offer the use of U.S. facilities for training purposes.

V. Command and Control of U.S. Forces

A. Our Policy: The President retains and will never relinquish command authority over U.S. forces. On a case by case basis, the President will consider placing appropriate U.S. forces under the operational control of a competent UN commander for specific UN operations authorized by the Security Council. The greater the U.S. military role, the less likely it will be that the U.S. will agree to have a UN commander exercise overall operational control over U.S. forces. Any large scale participation of U.S. forces in a major peace enforcement mission that is likely to involve combat should ordinarily be conducted under U.S. command and operational control or through competent regional organizations such as NATO or ad hoc coalitions.

There is nothing new about this Administration's policy regarding the command and control of U.S. forces. U.S. military personnel have participated in UN peace operations since 1948. American forces have served under the operational control of foreign commanders since the Revolutionary War, including in World War I, World War II, Operation Desert Storm and in NATO since its inception. We have done so and will continue to do so when the President determines it serves U.S. national interests.

Since the end of the Cold War, U.S. military personnel have begun serving in UN operations in greater numbers. President Bush sent a large U.S. field hospital unit to Croatia and observers to Cambodia, Kuwait and Western Sahara. President Clinton has deployed two U.S. infantry companies to Macedonia in a monitoring capacity and logisticians to the UN operation in Somalia.

B. Definition of Command: No President has ever relinquished command over U.S. forces. Command constitutes the authority to issue orders covering every aspect of military operations and administration. The sole source of legitimacy for U.S. commanders originates from the U.S. Constitution, federal law and the Uniform Code of Military Justice and flows from the President to the lowest U.S. commander in the field. The chain of command from the President to the lowest U.S. commander in the field remains inviolate.

C. Definition of Operational Control: It is sometimes prudent or advantageous (for reasons such as maximizing military effectiveness and ensuring unity of command) to place U.S. forces under the operational control of a foreign commander to achieve specified military objectives. In making this determination, factors such as the mission, the size of the proposed U.S. force, the risks involved, anticipated duration, and rules of engagement will be carefully considered.

Operational control is a subset of command. It is given for a specific time frame or mission and includes the authority to assign tasks to U.S. forces already deployed by the President, and assign tasks to U.S. units led by U.S. officers. Within the limits of operational control, a foreign UN commander cannot: change the mission or deploy U.S. forces outside the area of responsibility agreed to by the President, separate units, divide their supplies, administer discipline, promote anyone, or change their internal organization.

D. Fundamental Elements of U.S. Command Always Apply: If it is to our advantage to place U.S. forces under the operational control of a UN commander, the fundamental elements of U.S. command still apply. U.S. commanders will maintain the capability to report separately to higher U.S. military authorities, as well as the UN commander. Commanders of U.S. military units participating in UN operations will refer to higher U.S. authorities orders that are illegal under U.S. or international law, or are outside the mandate of the mission to which the U.S. agreed with the UN, if they are unable to resolve the matter with the UN commander. The U.S. reserves the right to terminate participation at any time and to take whatever actions it deems necessary to protect U.S. forces if they are endangered.

There is no intention to use these conditions to subvert the operational chain of command. Unity of command remains a vital concern. Questions of legality, mission mandate, and prudence will continue to be worked out "on the ground" before the orders are issued. The U.S. will continue to work with the UN and other member states to streamline command and control procedures and maximize effective coordination on the ground.

E. Protection of U.S. Peacekeepers: The U.S. remains concerned that in some cases, captured UN peacekeepers and UN peace enforcers may not have adequate protection under international law. The U.S. believes that individuals captured while performing UN peacekeeping or UN peace enforcement activities, whether as members of a UN force or a U.S. force executing a UN Security Council mandate, should, as a matter of policy, be immediately released to UN officials; until released, at a minimum they should be accorded protections identical to those afforded prisoners of war under the 1949 Geneva Convention III (GPW). The U.S. will generally seek to incorporate appropriate language into UN Security Council resolutions that establish or extend peace operations in order to provide adequate legal protection to captured UN peacekeepers. In appropriate cases, the U.S. would seek assurances that U.S. forces assisting the UN are treated as experts on mission for the United Nations, and thus are entitled to appropriate privileges and immunities and are subject to immediate release when captured. Moreover, the Administration is actively involved in negotiating a draft international convention at the United Nations to provide a special international status for individuals serving in peacekeeping and peace enforcement operations under a UN mandate. Finally, the Administration will take appropriate steps to ensure that any U.S. military personnel captured while serving as part of a multinational peacekeeping force or peace enforcement effort are immediately released to UN authorities.

VI. Strengthening U.S. Support for Multilateral Peace Operations

Peace operations have changed since the end of the Cold War. They are no longer limited to the interposition of small numbers of passive, unarmed observers. Today, they also include more complex and sometimes more robust uses of military resources to achieve a range of political and humanitarian objectives.

The post-Cold War world has also witnessed the emergence of peace enforcement operations involving the threat or use of force. These missions have been considerably more challenging than traditional peacekeeping operations, yet the U.S. and the UN are only now beginning to change sufficiently the way they manage peace operations.

The expansion of peacekeeping operations without a commensurate expansion of capabilities has contributed to noticeable setbacks. If the U.S. is to support the full range of peace operations effectively, when it is in our interests to do so, our government, not just the UN, must adapt. It is no longer sufficient to view peace operations solely through a political prism. It is critical also to bring a clear military perspective to bear, particularly on those missions that are likely to involve the use of force or the participation of U.S. combat units. Thus, the Department of Defense should join the Department of State in assuming both policy and funding responsibility for appropriate peace operations. We call this policy shared responsibility.

A. Shared Responsibility: DOD will assume new responsibilities for managing and funding those UN peace operations that are likely to involve combat and all operations in which U.S. combat units are participating. The military requirements of these operations demand DOD's leadership in coordinating U.S. oversight and management. Professional military judgement increases the prospects of success of such operations. Moreover, with policy management responsibility comes funding responsibility.

DOD will pay the UN assessment for those traditional UN peacekeeping missions (so called Chapter VI operations, because they operate under Chapter VI of the UN Charter) in which U.S. combat units are participating, e.g. Macedonia. DOD will also pay the UN assessment for all UN peace enforcement missions (so called "Chapter VII" operations), e.g. Bosnia and Somalia.

State will continue to manage and pay for traditional peacekeeping missions in which there are no U.S. combat units participating, e.g. Golan Heights, El Salvador, Cambodia. When U.S. military personnel, goods or services are used for UN peace operations, DOD will receive direct and full reimbursement; reimbursement can only be waived in exceptional circumstances, and only by the President.

Our Shared Responsibility policy states: Unless the President determines otherwise, at the request of one of the Principals:

— The State Department will have lead responsibility for the oversight and management of those traditional peacekeeping operations (Chapter VI) in which U.S. combat units are not participating. The Administration will seek to fund the assessments for these operations through the existing State Contributions for International Peacekeeping Activities account, and;

— The Defense Department will have lead responsibility for the oversight and management of those Chapter VI operations in which there are U.S. combat units and for all peace enforcement (Chapter VII) peace operations. The Administration will seek to fund the assessments for these operations through the establishment of a new account within DOD established to pay UN assessments. Once such an account is established, DOD may receive direct reimbursement from the UN for contributions of goods, services, and troops to UN peace operations.

The Administration will submit legislation to Congress creating a new peacekeeping assessment account for DOD and implementing the shared responsibility concept. The legislation will stipulate that, in all cases, the agency with lead responsibility for a given operation will be responsible for assessments associated with the operation. Since peace operations are neither wholly military nor wholly political in nature, consisting instead of military, political, humanitarian and developmental elements in varying degrees, no one agency alone can manage all facets of an operation effectively. Therefore, the designated lead agencies will engage in full and regular interagency consultation as they manage U.S. support for peace operations.

In all cases, State remains responsible for the conduct of diplomacy and instructions to embassies and our UN Mission in New York.

DOD is responsible for military assessments and activities. NSC facilitates interagency coordination.

B. Reimbursements from the UN: Under the shared responsibility policy, and the proposed accompanying legal authorities, DOD would receive and retain direct reimbursement for its contributions of troops, goods and services to the UN. An important advantage will be to limit any adverse impact on

DOD Operations and Maintenance funds, which are essential to the U.S. military readiness. As our draft legislation stipulates, the U.S. will seek full reimbursement from the UN for U.S. contributions of troops, goods and services. The U.S. will first apply reimbursements against DOD incremental costs. Any remaining excess after the Services have been made whole would be credited to DOD's proposed peace-keeping account when it is a DOD-led operation or to State's CIPA account when it is a State-led operation. The President may choose to waive UN reimbursement only in exceptional circumstances.

C. U.S. Funding of UN Peace Operations: In the short term, the Administration will seek Congressional support for funding the USG's projected UN peacekeeping arrears. Over the long run, we view the shared responsibility approach outlined above as the best means of ensuring improved management and adequate funding of UN peace operations. Moreover, the Administration will make every effort to budget for known peacekeeping assessments and seek Congressional support to fund, in the annual appropriation, assessments for clearly anticipated contingencies.

D. U.S. Training: The Armed Services will include appropriate peacekeeping/emergency humanitarian assistance training in DOD training programs. Training U.S. forces to fight and decisively win wars will, however, continue to be the highest training priority.

VII. Congress and the American People

To sustain U.S. support for UN peace operations, Congress and the American people must understand and accept the potential value of such operations as tools of U.S. interests. Congress and the American people must also be genuine participants in the processes that support U.S. decision-making on new and on-going peace operations. Traditionally, the Executive branch has not solicited the involvement of

Congress or the American people on matters related to UN peacekeeping. This lack of communication is not desirable in an era when peace operations have become more numerous, complex and expensive. The Clinton Administration is committed to working with Congress to improve and regularize communication and consultation on these important issues. Specifically, the Administration will:

— Regularize recently-initiated periodic consultations with bipartisan Congressional leaders on foreign policy engagements that might involve U.S. forces, including possible deployments of U.S. military units in UN peace operations.

— Continue recently-initiated monthly staff briefings on the UN's upcoming calendar, including current, new, and expanded peace operations.

— Inform Congress as soon as possible of unanticipated votes in the UNSC on new or expanded peace operations.

— Inform Congress of UN command and control arrangements when U.S. military units participate in UN operations.

— Provide UN documents to appropriate committees on a timely basis.

— Submit to Congress a comprehensive annual report on UN peace operations.

— Support legislation along the lines of that introduced by Senators Mitchell, Nunn, Byrd and Warner to amend the War Powers Resolution to introduce a consultative mechanism and to eliminate the 60-day withdrawal provisions.

Conclusion

Properly constituted, peace operations can be one useful tool to advance American national interests and pursue our national security objectives. The U.S. cannot be the world's policeman. Nor can we ignore the increase in armed ethnic conflicts, civil wars and the collapse of governmental authority in some states — crises that individually and cumulatively may affect U.S. interests. This policy is designed to impose discipline on both the UN and the U.S. to make peace operations a more effective instrument of collective security.

U.S. Department of State Publication Number 10161 Released by the Bureau of International Organization Affairs May 1994.

TO AMEND TITLE 10, UNITED STATES CODE, TO PROHIBIT ANY MEMBER OF THE ARMED FORCES FROM BEING REQUIRED TO WEAR AS PART OF THE MILITARY UNIFORM ANY INDICIA OR INSIGNIA OF THE UNITED NATIONS. (INTRODUCED IN THE HOUSE)

HR 2540 IH

104th CONGRESS

1st Session

H. R. 2540

To amend title 10, United States Code, to prohibit any member of the Armed Forces from being required to wear as part of the military uniform any indicia or insignia of the United Nations.

IN THE HOUSE OF REPRESENTATIVES

October 26, 1995

Mr. DELAY (for himself, Mr. FIELDS of Texas, Mr. HASTERT, Mr. EWING, Mr. STUMP, Mrs. CHENOWETH, Mr. FUNDERBURK, Mr. CRANE, Mr. STOCKMAN, Mr. ROHRABACHER, and Mr. HAYWORTH) introduced the following bill; which was referred to the Committee on National Security

A BILL

To amend title 10, United States Code, to prohibit any member of the Armed Forces from being required to wear as part of the military uniform any indicia or insignia of the United Nations.

Be it enacted by the Senate and House of Representatives of the United States of America in Congress assembled,

SECTION 1. PROHIBITION ON REQUIREMENT FOR MEMBERS OF THE ARMED FORCES TO WEAR UNIFORM ITEMS OF THE UNITED NATIONS.

(a) IN GENERAL- Chapter 45 of title 10, United States Code, is amended by adding at the end the following new section:

`Sec. 777. Insignia of United Nations: prohibition on requirement for wearing

`No member of the armed forces may be required to wear as part of the uniform any badge, symbol, helmet, headgear, or other visible indicia or insignia which indicates (or tends to indicate) any allegiance or affiliation to or with the United Nations.'.

(b) CLERICAL AMENDMENT- The table of sections at the beginning of such chapter is amended by adding at the end the following new item:

`777. Insignia of United Nations: prohibition on requirement for wearing.'.

CONDEMNING THE DEPLOYMENT OF UNITED STATES MILITARY PERSONNEL IN THE SERVICE OF THE UNITED NATIONS IN THE FORMER YUGOSLAV REPUBLIC OF MACEDONIA. (INTRODUCED IN THE HOUSE)

HCON 158 IH

105th CONGRESS

1st Session

H. CON. RES. 158

Condemning the deployment of United States military personnel in the service of the United Nations in the former Yugoslav Republic of Macedonia.

IN THE HOUSE OF REPRESENTATIVES

September 25, 1997

Mrs. CHENOWETH (for herself, Mr. BARTLETT of Maryland, and Mr. HALL of Texas) submitted the following concurrent resolution; which was referred to the Committee on International Relations, and in addition to the Committee on National Security, for a period to be subsequently determined by the Speaker, in each case for consideration of such provisions as fall within the jurisdiction of the committee concerned.

CONCURRENT RESOLUTION

Condemning the deployment of United States military personnel in the service of the United Nations in the former Yugoslav Republic of Macedonia.

Whereas Article I, Section 9, Clause 8 of the Constitution of the United States prohibits any person holding an office of profit or trust under the United States from accepting any office from a foreign government without the consent of Congress;

Whereas all Federal employees, including all military personnel, hold offices of profit or trust under the United States;

Whereas the United Nations has been construed to be a `foreign government' under section 7342 of title 5, United States Code, a provision of law that prohibits the acceptance of gifts or decorations by Federal employees from foreign governments;

Whereas the United Nations Participation Act of 1945 expressly prohibits the President from deploying United States military personnel in service of the United Nations for actions taken under Chapter VII of the United Nations Charter without the approval of Congress;

Whereas United Nations resolutions concerning all deployments in the former Yugoslavia, including the former Yugoslav Republic of Macedonia, have relied upon Chapter VII of the United Nations Charter for its authority for the deployment of troops;

Whereas President Clinton has deployed United States military personnel to this battle-torn region and such personnel have been ordered to assume the additional office of `U.N. soldier';

Whereas all officers who command United Nations forces take the following oath of exclusive loyalty to the United Nations: `I solemnly affirm to exercise in all loyalty, discretion and conscience the functions entrusted to me as a member of the international service of the United Nations, to discharge those functions and regulate my conduct with the interest of the United Nations only in view, and not to seek or accept instructions in respect to the performance of my duties from any government or other authority external to the organization';

Whereas Congress has not consented to the deployment of United States military personnel to the former Yugoslav Republic of Macedonia as required by the United Nations Participation Act of 1945;

Whereas it is the inherent right of every United States citizen to maintain a singular loyalty to this Nation;

Whereas it has been the high privilege and honor of many of our bravest citizens to serve alongside the military of other nations, but it is a grave violation of the rights of a citizen-soldier to coerce that soldier to become a member of any military other than that of the United States;

Whereas any legislative mandate ordering the President to comply with the applicable law may place United States servicemen and servicewomen into unnecessary difficulties; and

Whereas the Congress believes the best interest of both our Nation and our military personnel necessitates a deliberate path in seeking voluntary compliance with the law by the President: Now, therefore, be it

Resolved by the House of Representatives (the Senate concurring), That the Congress—

(1) condemns the deployment of United States military personnel in the service of the United Nations in the former Yugoslav Republic of Macedonia as a violation of both the Constitution and the laws of the United States;

(2) calls upon the President to perform his constitutional duty as Commander-in-Chief by forthwith taking total command of all United States military personnel

participating in United Nations operations, to take the appropriate steps to ensure that United States military personnel wear only the uniform of the United States without any items from the United Nations, and to carry military identity cards issued by the United States only and not by the United Nations; and

(3) calls upon the President to take expeditiously all steps necessary to resolve all existing conflicts with United States military personnel who have bravely stood for the right to be exclusively loyal to this Nation and who have refused to serve under foreign commanders in foreign uniforms consistent with the constitutional and principles of this resolution.

REMARKS OF MICHAEL G. NEW
MICHAEL NEW HOMECOMING RALLY
MONTGOMERY COUNTY COURTHOUSE
CONROE, TEXAS
JULY 28, 1996

Standing is an important posture in life. People stand when the national anthem is played. When the flag passes, people stand and cover their hearts. On political issues people ask where do you stand, what is your position? For generations, parents in America have taught us how to stand. They have shown us what to stand for and what to stand against.

I am here today for no other reason than the fact that I made a stand as a U.S. Army Specialist on October 10, 1995. It was a simple act. The course set before me was clear. I had no question about where to stand that early fall morning in Schweinfurt, Germany.

It all began on August 21, 1995 when my seniors in the U.S. Army chain of command informed me that my battalion, First of the Fifteenth, 3rd Infantry Division, would soon be deployed to a UN operation in Macedonia. However, they said this UN mission would be different from the previous UN mission on which I served in Kuwait. My seniors informed me that this deployment required my battalion to significantly alter our uniforms by removing the U.S. flag from the right shoulder, the senior side of the U.S. Army Battle Dress Uniform, to the left shoulder, and replace the flag with a UN patch, badge and insignia. We would also wear a UN blue beret or helmet.

This seemed like an unusual requirement, to put the UN badge in a more important position on my uniform than the flag. Without knowing a lot about the UN, it seemed wrong to me. The Army taught me that the wearing of a uniform, or the accoutrements of a uniform, was a sign of allegiance and faithfulness to the authority or power so signified. As an American fighting man, how could I wear the badges and insignia of another government? I had taken an oath to the United States of America and no other. I had sworn to support and defend the Constitution against all enemies foreign and domestic, to obey the orders of the President and those in authority over me. But the Army enlisted oath doesn't bind me to blind obedience, but goes on to say "according to regulations and the Uniform Code of Military Justice, so help me, God."

Like I said in that oath, I fully intended to obey all lawful orders, according to regulations. Congress makes all regulations governing the land and naval forces. And the experts in the military on the wearing of the regulation uniform are the sergeants. So, I asked my sergeant, how we as American soldiers, could wear a "UN uniform" and still be American soldiers? The response I got to my sergeant's level question about the proper wear of the historic U.S. Army uniform was not what I expected. I was threatened with court martial, imprisonment or less than an honorable discharge, if I did not wear the "UN uniform."

And further, I was directed to study the history and objectives of the UN. This I did and I was more proud to be an American than ever before. I knew I did not want to be a member of the UN military force. The UN Charter, their constitution, is based upon very subjective man-made regulations and their brand of human rights are given by the men of the United Nations. Their rights are not like those we have been endowed with by our Creator, but rather can be modified or taken away by the UN. I saw from my own study that the UN's authority and founding principles are diametrically opposed to the founding documents of America, my country, and the United States, my government.

As the time ticked off from August, through September to October, I did not receive an answer from the Army about the lawfulness of the order to wear the badges and insignia of the UN on my uniform, until October 2, 1995, when there was a special unprecedented briefing on the legal basis for deployment to Macedonia and the wearing of the "UN uniform." The five hundred and fifty soldiers in my battalion filed into an auditorium in Schweinfurt to hear from an Army lawyer, who was a West Point graduate. At the end of a 52 minute presentation, he finally came to the answer I had been waiting so many tense weeks to hear. The reason, he says, we wear the UN uniform, is because "they look fabulous!" Everyone in the auditorium laughed. I didn't think it was very funny.

By that time I knew that the UN uniform was not regulation. The only regulation berets are the Green for Special Forces, the black for Rangers and the maroon for Airborne. None of the seven UN uniform accoutrements have made it into the Army's regulation handbook for soldiers because Congress has not approved the wear of the UN uniform.

My stand was not a matter of conscience, it was a matter of my understanding that there is an objective standard which doesn't make allowances for what I think or feel about it. I believe that the laws and our Constitution are the final word, and I had sworn to uphold this objective external standard. Thus on October 10, 1995, on a misty fall morning, I walked out into a sea of baby blue, in my historic and completely regulation U.S. Army battle dress uniform. The same uniform in which many a brave soldier has shed blood in order to preserve and protect our American way of life. I was ordered to fall out for not surrendering my regulation BDU. As I followed my squad leader from the formation that October day, I knew I would never return to my unit and that I was in trouble with a huge institution, one which I care a great deal about, and one in which I strove to be a good soldier.

After I made my intention to stand firm clear to my family, Dad knew I was going to need some legal assistance. My mother and father have been very supportive throughout and I can never thank them enough for standing by each other all these years and especially for standing by me over the past year. They taught me that in life taking a stand could cost me. They were right.

Dad found help for me in Colonel Ronald D. Ray. A retired Marine, Col. Ray is a lawyer, a Vietnam combat veteran and an historian. I received word that I would be court martialed for my stand and Colonel Ray began researching my legal position. He said my stand did not just need a defense. It also needed an offense. He said, "We never win on the defense. We must take the war to them." While he told me my case was conclusive, and that I was on solid legal ground, he did not trust the courts. And, as a Vietnam veteran, he said experience had taught him that you can win all the battles and yet lose the war in the court of public opinion. Therefore Colonel Ray and my father took the offensive war to the airwaves of talk radio and let people know of my stand.

I believe that Colonel Ray was ignited by my stand but he also said he had a belly full of limited "no-win" UN wars, probably from his time in Vietnam. Some of you may be veterans of the Korean war. Korea was the first limited UN war in which victory was not the primary objective. Orders began coming from New York instead of Washington and General MacArthur, who said, "In war there is no substitute for victory," had to be relieved of command. That kind of winning attitude had to be eliminated. Then came Vietnam. It badly marked a generation. Men, deceived by their political leaders, fought half a world away when the real battle was being fought here for the heart and soul of America. It seemed, as I learned more about how the UN military wages "peace" in places like Korea, Vietnam, and Somalia, that Macedonia and

Bosnia seemed like more of the same limited "no-win" UN wars.

In January 1996 as we prepared for court martial, my stand would ratchet up in a way I could never have anticipated due to four Presidential letters which appeared in Col. Ray's fax machine from Germany late one evening. These letters were part of the legal discovery the Army owed my defense but they were held back without comment and too late for inclusion in the written legal presentation before the court. These letters would show without question that Bill Clinton had misrepresented the Macedonian deployment to Congress. Mr. Clinton told the Congress in those four letters that the Macedonian mission was not of significant danger to warrant their approval. That was provably not true. The Colonel said that the military judge would never rule on the lawfulness of a Presidential order, so he filed suit against the Secretary of Defense and the Secretary of the Army seeking an honorable discharge for me in an independent federal court. The offensive campaign in the Courts, the Congress and the court of public opinion was really accelerating.

The President said the Macedonian deployment was a Chapter VI UN mission. However, 27 UN Security Council Resolutions would refer to the Macedonian deployment as a Chapter VII, which, under the UN Participation Act of 1945, requires Congressional approval. Approval is required because the Constitution provided for a balance of power. The President is not a King. When America sends her sons and daughters into harms way, the voice and will of "We the People" must be heard through our elected representatives. This responsibility and limitation on his Presidential authority was something else Bill Clinton dodged. I clearly understood my stand was now toe to toe with Bill Clinton. On October 10, 1995, my stand was related to my change of status as an American fighting man. I had not questioned foreign policy. Remember, I had asked a sergeant's level question.

1. I was standing against an unlawful order to deploy to Macedonia; 2. refusing the President's order to wear the UN uniform; 3. refusing to serve under a foreign UN commander; 4. and refusing to be required to carry only the UN identification card.

In January 1995, as a result of the Presidential letters, my stand began to be seen in a much larger context, as a stand for the country and a stand for over 30,000 other soldiers unlawfully deployed around the world in UN military operations.

However, on January 24, 1996, I was convicted of not obeying what the prosecution called a "lawful order" even though they admitted in open court in Germany that the uniform was not a regulation uniform. My defense was not allowed to put on the overwhelming evidence that the order was unlawful which pointed to presidential wrongdoing and the failure of Congressional oversight. The military judge basically said it was above his pay grade to rule on Presidential wrong doing and bucked it up to the next judiciary level.

My stand has brought me back to America with a Bad Conduct Discharge and appeals hanging over me in both the civilian and military court systems. I left Germany in the middle of July and traveled to Washington to meet with Congressional leaders whom Colonel Ray had briefed on my stand and its significance to American law and public policy. Because of my stand and the tremendous support my stand has received from many wonderful people like you, Colonel Ray gained access to testify before a Senate foreign policy subcommittee and UN ambassador Madeline Albright had to come and explain by what authority America soldiers are transferred from the U.S. military to the UN military. Through it all, I have simply stood and, until reaching America two weeks ago, I have not spoken about this matter, which shows just how powerful a stand can be.

I am now out of uniform, but the Congress is not out of jeopardy of losing control of America's military to U.N. command and control. But because of my stand, there is legislation now in Congress. H.R. 3308, which is deceptively entitled, "The Armed Forces Protection Act of 1996," has been rightly labeled by Congressman Roscoe Bartlett as "unconstitutional, containing an illegal transfer of Congressional authority to the Executive branch."

If it is passed, H.R. 3308 will give legislative and political cover to President Clinton for his three years of misrepresentation to Congress in sending U.S. soldiers like me on UN military operations to places like Macedonia, forcing us to wear unauthorized UN uniforms, and to serve under foreign UN commanders. These UN commanders take an oath of exclusive allegiance to the United Nations, but after committing themselves to the UN and being put on the UN payroll, they command U.S. troops making life and death decisions over them.

Even President Clinton has admitted that if captured, these troops, unlawfully deployed, fall into a legal quagmire in international law when serving as UN military. They lose important legal protections if taken hostage, as many have been in Macedonia, and that is of critical importance, especially if the one captured is your son, father, uncle, or anyone else in your family.

Substitute legislation has been drafted and offered by my defense team to Congressmen and women to introduce and support in opposition to H.R. 3308. It is entitled "The American Soldier Protection and American Command Preservation Act." It would prevent the president and others from freely internationalizing the U.S. armed forces through the multi-national government of the United Nations. I am told the Republicans have been slow to pick up this legislation and the opportunity to shame Bill Clinton for this bad treatment of American soldiers, especially in an election year. Col. Ray says it is because they don't really disagree with Clinton's UN policies to wage "peace" around the world.

Now, as you can tell, I am not a speaker or a politician. I am a soldier. I swore an oath to the Constitution, took my post and I made my stand. I was proud and comforted to make my stand on October 10, 1995, protected by our Constitution. I have done what I am able to do. Let my stand serve as a sign to you of how far we have gone in subjugating the United States military to the United Nations military. However, I must tell you I do not intend to become a symbol, only a sign to point out, in this case, a hazard. I do not want to be held up as something extraordinary. I did only what I had to do to be able to keep my oath and live with myself.

The message I stand before you today to give you is to contact the Legal Defense Fund, keep up with the latest information in regard to the defense of my stand, which so many of you have kindly adopted. My mission in the courts is simply to obtain an honorable discharge for my honorable disobedience.

Also, please stay current with the offensive action taken as a result of my stand, the Congressional legislation developed by Colonel Ray and others more skilled than I, to protect our country and support our troops. If I could cause this much trouble as one person, just think about what you can do. It is up to you.

I am a simple soldier, and I am now a civilian, as I said earlier, I am not a speaker or a politician, but there are those of you who are. And because you are, I charge you this day to take up this effort because the day is coming soon when the U.S. Army Code of Conduct will become as obsolete as General MacArthur became during the Korean war when the code was written I am told by heroes like Duane Thorin, because of the confusion among the ranks about their allegiance: To the UN or U.S? It reads in part:

"I will never forget that I am an American fighting man. I serve in the forces which guard my country and our way of life. I am prepared to give my life in their defense.

"I will never surrender of my own free will. If in command I will never surrender my men while they still have the means to resist.

"I will never forget that I am an American fighting man, responsible for my actions, and dedicated to the principles which make my country free. I will trust in God and in the United States of America."

Thank you, God bless you and God bless America.

Resolutions of Support

ROLLING THUNDER INC.

Rolling Thunder, Inc., an active veterans organization which focuses on POW/MIA and veterans' issues, has recently passed the following resolution:

"A great many of our number have served in our country's military. They all took the same oath to obey the orders of their superiors, to protect and defend this Great Nation.

"There is not a member in our ranks who was ever called upon to take an oath to the United Nations, and if they were, they would not have taken it.

"For, by taking their oath, they agreed to wear this and only this Nation's uniform and symbols, not the uniform and symbols of other nations. They agreed to take the orders of their superiors within the military services and the Commanders In Chief of this nation.

"They did not agree to take orders of leaders of other Nations or their military. It is one thing to respect the superiors of other Nations, but it is indeed another matter to obey their commands.

"We do not believe that the Constitution has been amended to allow the Commander in Chief to force citizens of this

Nation to wear the uniform of another nation such as the United Nations.

"As such, we believe that this soldier, Michael New, has been mistreated badly by his superiors and denied the due process required by our Constitution and the Bill of Rights."

(signed) October 9, 1998

THE DAILY RECORD

"Serving under a mongrel flag doesn't appeal to U.S. soldier"

by Paul Harvey

The only time I ever took on the United States Army was more than 50 years ago. I neither lost nor won.

With the flying experience that I had gained since I was 16, I enlisted as an Air Force cadet — only to be informed weeks later that the cadet program had been abolished and that all cadet trainees were being transferred to regular Army.

All cadets were distressed, none more than I.

What we did not know — and what the Army could not tell us — was that this was no reflection on our flying potential. It was just that President Eisenhower was planning a multiple invasion of the continent of Europe and he needed masses of grunts more than he needed fly boys.

For obvious reasons, the Air Force did not want a court challenge of whether an Air Force volunteer could summarily be transferred to another branch of service. Before long, I was a civilian again and eligible to be drafted, but it was soon thereafter we ran out of war.

That experience helps me now to understand Army Specialist Michael New. This American soldier now stationed in Germany does not believe our government has a constitutional right to enlist him in a peace-keeping force for the United Nations.

He volunteered to serve the United States and the American flag.

He is resisting transfer to a hybrid international force under a mongrel flag.

New has been informed that his unit is to be deployed in Macedonia as part of a U.N. "peace-keeping" contingent there. There, American soldiers will be required to wear U.N. insignias on their uniforms and serve under a foreign U.N. commander.

He has been advised that his unwillingness to wear a "foreign uniform" may subject him to court martial for "disobeying a legal order."

He told *The New American*, "I explained to my lieutenant that I don't think I should have to wear a U.N. arm band or A U.N. beret. I enlisted in the Army of the United States; I am not a U.N. soldier. I have taken no vow to the U.N. I have taken an oath to defend the Constitution of the United States against all enemies, foreign and domestic. Where does my oath say that I have an obligation to the U.N.?"

New has told his superiors that he believes the U.N. to be "a foreign power, no different from a foreign government." He says he would also refuse to wear a Russian uniform or salute a Russian flag.

Retired Marine Corps Colonel Ronald D. Ray, a former deputy assistant secretary of Defense, is providing legal counsel to the New family. He says that New has been the victim of a "bait and switch." He was recruited to serve the red, white and blue — not the U.N. Further, as a U.S. soldier, he could be held captive as a hostage."

To shuck down to the cob: "U.S. law provides no specific guidelines for U.S. military under U.N. command."

Ray says New has focused attention on a question of tremendous historic importance.

Paul Harvey is a nationally syndicated columnist with Creators Syndicate.

In the

UNITED STATES ARMY COURT OF CRIMINAL APPEALS

Docket No. ARMY 9600263

United States,

Appellee

v.

Specialist Michael G. New,
United States Army,

Appellant.

REPLY BRIEF ON BEHALF OF APPELLANT

HENRY L. HAMILTON, P.A.
Civilian Appellate Defense Counsel
Ratchford & Associates
1531 Laurel Street
Columbia, SC 29201-2697
(803) 779-0700

PAUL FIORINO
Captain, JA
Appellate Defense Counsel
5611 Columbia Pike
Falls Church, VA 22041
(703) 681-3593

TABLE OF CONTENTS

<u>Assignment of Error IX and Reply Argument</u>

TABLE OF AUTHORITIES CITED

B. <u>U.S. COURT OF APPEALS FOR THE ARMED
FORCES.</u>

III. STATUTES AND REGULATIONS.

IN THE UNITED STATES ARMY COURT OF CRIMINAL APPEALS

UNITED STATES, Appellee	))))	REPLY BRIEF ON BEHALF OF APPELLANT
	)	Docket No. ARMY 9600263
v.	)	
	)	Tried at Leighton Barracks,
Specialist **Michael G. New**, United States Army, Appellant	))))	Wuerzburg, Germany on 24 October, 17 November, 8 and 13 December, 1995 and 18, 19, 23, and 24 January, 1996 before a Special Court-Martial Empowered to Adjudge a Bad Conduct Discharge appointed by the Commander, 3d Infantry Division, LTC W. Gary Jewell, military judge, presiding.

TO THE HONORABLE, THE JUDGES OF THE UNITED
STATES ARMY COURT OF CRIMINAL APPEALS

Statement of the Case

The appellant filed assignments of error with this Court on
3 July 1997. On 5 February 1998 the government answered
appellant's assignments of error. On 11 February 1998 appellant moved to extend the deadline for filing the present reply

to the government's answer. On 19 February 1998 this Court granted appellant's motion for an extension of time to reply to the government's answer.

Statement of Facts

Those facts necessary to a disposition of the assigned errors are set forth in the Brief on Behalf of Appellant and in the arguments, *infra*.

Reply to the Government's Answer[1]

I

THE MILITARY JUDGE ABUSED HIS DISCRETION BY DENYING SPC NEW'S CAUSAL CHALLENGE AGAINST A MEMBER WHO ORDERED A SUBORDINATE TO WEAR THE UN UNIFORM AND DEPLOY TO MACEDONIA.

The government's brief correctly notes that challenges for cause should be liberally granted. (Resp. Br. at 3). However, the government's brief misinterprets several issues with respect to actual and implied bias.

With respect to actual bias, the government contends that the defense theory for excluding COL Kwist was insufficient (Id.) because the defense did not establish whether COL Kwist ever ordered his subordinate captain to deploy to Macedonia. (Resp. Br. at 4). However, focusing on whether COL Kwist personally ordered his captain to deploy to Macedonia misses the point. The defense clearly established that COL Kwist had been ordered by his superiors to identify and provide one of his captains for the Macedonia mission

---

[1] The appellant reasserts and invites the Court's examination of *Grostefon* Issue I. (App. Br. at A-1-1 through A-1-8.)

and that COL Kwist personally carried out that order or caused it to be carried out.[2] Thus, COL Kwist clearly had an interest in the seminal matter around which SPC New's court-martial revolved. Consequently, for COL Kwist to vote "not guilty" at SPC New's court-martial would require COL Kwist to impeach and affirmatively disavow the validity of the order COL Kwist received *after* COL Kwist had carried out that order or caused that order to be carried out. In light of COL Kwist's obvious interest in the outcome of the case, the military judge's denial of the defense challenge for cause against COL Kwist constituted an abuse of discretion.

The government also contends that COL Kwist was not confronted with precisely the identical situation presented by SPC New, i.e. the wearing of the UN Uniform (Resp. Br. at 4, note 2): "The assigned issue might have merit, had COL Kwist personally issued the same order to a subordinate, and then taken disciplinary action for that subordinate's refusal to wear the uniform." (Id.)

The government's contention in this regard is predicated on a hollow and immaterial distinction. COL Kwist's act of obeying his superiors' order to identify and provide a captain to deploy to Macedonia (R. at 533) clearly involved COL Kwist personally informing such captain that the captain was required to deploy to Macedonia or causing COL Kwist's subordinates to identify and inform such captain that the captain was required to deploy to Macedonia. In either event, COL Kwist was responsible for the order's execution. In addition, with the deployment instructions eventually came the collateral instruction for the captain to wear the UN Uniform. In other words, when COL Kwist received his superiors' order to identify and provide a captain to deploy to Macedonia, COL Kwist did not permit that order to languish in a state of limbo-like ambiguity without execution. Instead, he directly, or perhaps indirectly through his subordinates or staff, caused that

---

[2] The government does not contend that COL Kwist disobeyed his superiors' order.

order to be executed. Thus, he was personally involved with the identification and deployment of the captain which, in turn, involved the captain's donning the UN Uniform.

Furthermore, although COL Kwist denied any bias (R. at 532-533, Resp. Br. at 4), an appellate court need not accept as conclusive a challenged member's perfunctory disclaimer of personal interest or his *pro forma* assertion of impartiality. *United States v. Smart*, 21 M.J. 15 at 19 (C.M.A. 1985); *United States V. Harris*, 13 M.J. 288 (C.M.A. 1982). Such a legal fiction would strain the credulity of reasonable persons. With the defense having clearly made a case of actual bias, this Court should not rely on the bald assertions of COL Kwist that he could remain impartial notwithstanding his involvement in identifying and providing a captain for deployment to Macedonia in the UN Uniform.

With respect to implied bias, the government correctly notes that this Court views such matters from the perspective of a member of the public. *United States v. Minyard*, 46 M.J. 229 (1997). In setting forth an objective test for implied bias, *Minyard* made several points which are relevant to this case.

First, while *United States v. Moyar*, 24 M.J. 635 (A.C.M.R. 1987) refers to special deference provided to the military judge (Id. at 638, Resp. Br. At 6[3]), *Minyard* states that a reviewing court should give less deference to the trial judge when matters of implied bias are concerned. 46 M.J. at 231. *Minyard* goes on to hold that where matters of implied bias are raised, a court-martial member's credibility is not dispositive. Id.

Secondly, the government contends that "within the context of COL Kwist's responses to the entire line of questioning, the record does not support that the military judge abused his discretion in declining to excuse COL Kwist" and again refers to "COL Kwist's forthright and matter of fact discussion on his views of the UN deployment," (Resp. Br. at 6). Due to the

---

[3] It is unclear whether the government's brief at page 6 is addressing actual or implied bias. Of course, any reference to COL Kwist's courtroom demeanor is irrelevant when addressing implied bias due to the objective nature of implied. *Minyard, supra*.

objective nature of implied bias, however, such factors are immaterial to an implied bias analysis.

Finally, with respect to implied bias, the government's brief asserts that

> Appellant's case does not justify the application of implied bias, especially as the fact that the alleged bias goes to the issue of lawfulness of the order to wear the UN uniform, an issue that COL Kwist was not required to decide given the military judge's ruling that the issue was an interlocutory matter.

(Resp. Br. at 5.)

This observation again misses the point. Implied bias does not hinge on whether the order to wear the UN Uniform was lawful, or whether the military judge ruled on that issue. Implied bias hinges on whether, from the perspective of a reasonable member of the public, a senior commander who identified and sent his subordinate captain to Macedonia wearing a UN Uniform may properly sit in judgment of another soldier who is accused of refusing to do the same thing. Again, the issue involves the appearance of bias, and the standard is an objective one. *Minyard, supra.* For the same reasons that police officers and corrections officials have been historically excluded from sitting on criminal juries, COL Kwist "in the interest of having the court-martial free from substantial doubt as to legality, fairness, and impartiality"[4] should not have sat as a member at SPC New's court-martial.

II

THE EVIDENCE ADDUCED AT TRIAL WAS LEGALLY AND FACTUALLY INSUFFICIENT TO PROVE THAT SPC NEW FAILED TO OBEY A LAWFUL ORDER.

[4] R.C.M. 912 (f)(1)(N)

Appellant adheres to the discussion of this assignment of error set forth in his Brief on Behalf of Appellant.[5]

III

BECAUSE THE EVIDENCE AFTER THE GOVERNMENT'S CASE IN CHIEF SHOWED THAT SPC NEW WAS PREVENTED FROM COMPLYING WITH THE ORDER, THE MILITARY JUDGE ABUSED HIS DISCRETION BY FAILING TO GRANT THE DEFENSE MOTION FOR A FINDING OF NOT GUILTY.

Appellant adheres to the discussion of this assignment of error set forth in his Brief on Behalf of Appellant.[6]

IV

SPC NEW'S FIFTH AND SIXTH AMENDMENT RIGHTS TO DUE PROCESS AND A FAIR TRIAL WERE VIOLATED BECAUSE THE MILITARY JUDGE FAILED TO INSTRUCT THE MEMBERS ON THE DEFENSE OF INABILITY.

V

SPC NEW'S FIFTH AND SIXTH AMENDMENT RIGHTS TO DUE PROCESS AND A FAIR TRIAL WERE VIOLATED BECAUSE THE MILITARY JUDGE FAILED TO INSTRUCT THE MEMBERS ON THE DEFENSE OF OBEDIENCE TO ORDERS.

---

[5] With respect to any argument made in the government's answer to which the appellant does not reply in this pleading, the appellant reasserts his assignment of error and argument set forth in his Brief on Behalf of Appellant. Any inference that the appellant concedes that assignments of error or arguments set forth in the Brief on Behalf of Appellant lack merit is unwarranted.
[6] See previous footnote.

Combined Reply Argument for Assignments of
Error IV and V

The government brief focuses on a three-part test, enumerated by the then-named Court of Military Appeals in *United States v. Damatta-Olivera*, 37 M.J. 474 (C.M.A. l993),[7] to determine whether failure to give an instruction constitutes error. *Damatta-Olivera*, however, is completely inapposite to the issues raised in Assignments of Error IV and V; Assignments of Error IV and V deal with instructions on special defenses; *Damatta-Olivera* deals with a mere evidentiary instruction concerning a "defense-requested instruction on prior inconsistent statements... "37 M.J. at 478.

The cases cited under Assignments of Error IV and V in the Brief on Behalf of Appellant correctly set forth the methodology for determining whether the military judge must instruct on a special defense raised by the evidence. See also: R.C.M. 920(e)(3); R.C.M. 920, *Discussion*; R.C.M. 916(b); R.C.M. 916(d); R.C.M. 916(i); and Benchbook, para 5-10. The government's focus on *Damatta-Olivera* advocates a paradigm shift in evaluating whether special defense instructions must be given and suggests that existing law for special defense instructions has been superseded by the *Damatta-Olivera* test for evidentiary instructions. Assignments of Error IV and V do not address defense requests for evidentiary instructions pertaining to credibility of witnesses. Instead, Assignments of Error IV and V address instructions for special defenses which, once raised, require the government to prove beyond a reasonable doubt that such special defenses are not viable. Thus, special defenses raise matters of a "constitutional magnitude" and are entirely distinguishable from defense requests for evidentiary instructions about witness credibility. *United States v. Brooks*, 25 M.J. 175(C.M.A. 1987). See also *United*

---

[7] The test to determine if the denial of a requested instruction constitutes error is whether (1) the charge is correct; (2) 'it is not substantially covered in the main charge'; and (3) 'it is on such a vital point in the case that the failure to give it deprived defendant of a defense or seriously impaired its effective presentation.'" *Damatta-Olivera, supra*, 37 M.J. at 478 quoting *United States v. Winborn*, 14 USCMA 277, 282, 34 CMR 57, 62 (1963).

States v. Webster, 769 F.2d 487 (8th Cir. 1985) and *United States v. Hicks*, 748 F. 2d 854 (4th Cir. 1984).

As the Brief on Behalf of Appellant establishes, instructions on the defenses of inability and obedience to orders were required as a matter of law. The evidence clearly raised the defenses, and the military judge had a duty to instruct the members, *sua sponte*, on those defenses. R.C.M. 920(e)(3). (App. Br. at 14-20.) In arguing against this point, the government contends that "any requested instruction on inability and obedience to orders would be incorrect as a matter of law" (Resp. Br. at 13) and invites reference to previous discussion on those issues[8]. In any event, the government's *post hoc*, conclusory assertion that instructions on these special defenses would be incorrect is based on a flawed analysis of the issue. (Resp. Br. at 8,9.)

Instead of considering whether some evidence raised the defenses of inability and obedience to orders, the government, in order to advance its novel *Damatta-Olivera* test for special defenses, goes one step further and concludes that these special defenses would not have prevailed had the members been properly instructed. The issue, however, is whether the evidence raised these special defenses; if so, it was error for the military judge to fail to instruct on them. It is for the court-martial members to decide whether SPC New could prevail on the special defenses of inability and disobedience to orders.

In some general sense, the government contends that "the defense and issues in the case were adequately covered by the instructions given by the military judge to the members (R. 783-390)." (Resp. Br. at 11.) To the contrary, nowhere in the military judge's instructions does he even mention the special defense of inability. (R. at 782-784[9].)

---

[8] The government could be referring to the discussion on pages 7-10 of its brief in which Assignments of Error II (factual insufficiency) and III (failure to grant a motion for a finding of not guilty) are addressed.

[9] The government asserts that the special defenses of inability and obedience to orders were adequately covered in the instructions to the members which appear on pages 783-790 of the record of trial. (Resp. Br. at 11.) However, pages 784-790 of the record encompass instructions on burden of proof, circumstantial evidence, stipulations of fact and testimony, credibility of witnesses, character evidence, presumption of innocence, quanta of proof, and evaluation of evidence.

With respect to the special defense of obedience to orders, the military judge's instruction is garbled and confusing. The military judge instructed that "[w]hile the unlawfulness of an order or regulation is a defense to the charge of disobedience, the inherent emphasis in the military upon obedience, **except in cases where the order is patently illegal**, encourages compliance with orders irrespective of legality." (R. at 784) (emphasis added). This instruction essentially informs the members that, somewhere, this defense may exist, but only where the order is patently unlawful. Having repeatedly instructed the members that the order to wear the UN Uniform was lawful (R.782, 784), the military judge's instruction was essentially a command to convict SPC New. Furthermore, the instruction completely ignores the issue of obedience to lawful orders with respect to AR 670-1 as a defense to disobeying LTC Layfield.

Further still, the military judge's instructions completely ignore the defense of obedience to orders as it pertains to SPC New being ordered out of formation before the time for the order's compliance. Thus, the government's assertion that "the defenses and issues in the case were adequately covered by the instructions given by the military judge to the members" (Resp. Br. at 11) is wildly overplayed and clearly incorrect.

Even if this Court were to break new ground by applying *Damatta-Olivera* to special defenses, it remains clear that the military judge erred in failing to give instructions on the special defenses of inability and obedience to orders even under *Damatta-Olivera*'s three-prong conjunctive test.

With respect to the third prong of the *Damatta-Olivera* test, the government asserts that "[t]rial defense counsel's closing argument also demonstrates that that appellant's theory was placed before the members and appellant's defense was not hindered." (Resp. Br. at 13.) This misses the point; whether the defense counsel argues a particular theory is irrelevant under the third prong of the *Damatta-Olivera* test. *Damatta-Olivera*'s third prong looks to whether the requested instruction "is on **such a vital point in the case that the failure to give it deprived defendant of a defense** or seriously impaired its effective presentation." 37 M.J. at 478 (emphasis added). In light of the military judge's instruction to the members that the military judge is the only source of the law in the case (R. at 781), and his reminder that arguments of counsel are not evidence (Id.), any argument that counsel made does not adequately compensate for the military judge's lack of instruction on these two special defenses.

The special defenses of inability and obedience to orders were critical to SPC New's case. Without these special defenses, the only other defense available to SPC New would be to demonstrate that the order was not given, a proposition which could not be ethically or reasonably advanced. SPC New's special defenses were the very core, the absolute crux, of his defense. As such, the abject lack of instructions on such vital points deprived SPC New of his constitutional right to present his defense.

VI

SPC NEW'S FIFTH AND SIXTH AMENDMENT RIGHTS TO DUE PROCESS AND A FAIR TRIAL WERE VIOLATED BECAUSE THE MILITARY JUDGE INSTRUCTED THE MEMBERS ERRONEOUSLY ON THE DEFENSE OF MISTAKE.

Abuse of discretion can be shown where the challenged action is "arbitrary, fanciful, clearly unreasonable," or "clearly erroneous." *United States v. Mosely*, 42 M.J. 300, 303

(1995); *United States v. Travers*, 25 M.J. 61, 62 (C.M.A. 1987). The government contends that "[a]ppellant has failed to demonstrate that the military judge [sic] instructions were arbitrary, fanciful, clearly unreasonable, or clearly erroneous . . ." (Resp. Br. at 14.) As set forth on pages 20-24 of the Brief on Behalf of Appellant, however, the military judge's mistake instruction was "so convoluted, confusing, contradictory and erroneous that it violated SPC New's due process and fair trial rights." (App. Br. at 21.) The military judge's mistake instruction reads more like a prosecutor's closing argument or government appellate brief than a jury instruction. (R. at 784.)

First, the instruction was *arbitrary* because it unduly stressed the necessity to obey orders and had little, if anything, to do with the defense of mistake. (App. Br. at 21.)

Secondly, the instruction was *fanciful* because it introduced extraneous concepts like "patently illegal" and "immunity based on faithful obedience" without explaining or defining the terms and without disclosing the authority to which SPC New was required to be "faithfully obedien[t]." (App. Br. at 21-22.)

Thirdly, the instruction was *clearly unreasonable* because, after the military judge instructed the members that the possibility of a mistake defense existed, he then instructed them that, as a matter of law, it did not apply in SPC New's case. (App. Br. at 23.) As set forth in the Brief on Behalf of Appellant, the military judge's instruction was effectively a command to the members to convict SPC New.

Fourthly, the military judge's instruction was *clearly erroneous* in at least two respects: the military judge gave, within the context of a mistake instruction, a "reverse" obedience to orders instruction (App. Br. at 22); and the military judge's instruction improperly incorporated an inapplicable *mens rea* standard for the defense of mistake. (App. Br. at 23.)

Consequently, the government's assertion that "[a]ppellant

has failed to demonstrate that the military judge [sic] instructions were arbitrary, fanciful, clearly unreasonable, or clearly erroneous . . ." (Resp. Br. at 14) is conclusory, unmeritorious, and without basis.

VII

SPC NEW'S FIFTH AND SIXTH AMEND-MENT RIGHTS TO DUE PROCESS AND A FAIR TRIAL; HIS RIGHT TO A TRIAL BY MEMBERS; AND HIS RIGHTS TO COMPULSORY PROCESS, CONFRON-TATION OF WITNESSES, AND EFFECTIVE ASSISTANCE OF COUNSEL; WERE VIOLATED BECAUSE THE MILITARY JUDGE FAILED TO PERMIT THE MEMBERS TO HEAR EVIDENCE CONCERNING THE UNLAWFULNESS OF THE ORDER.

The government correctly notes that "[i]n a trial by jury, the jurors determine questions of fact..." (Resp. Br. at 24.) In answering Assignment of Error VII,[10] however, the government bases its argument on two outcome determinative assumptions: that the lawfulness of the order was clear as a matter of law, and that the determination concerning the lawfulness of the order did not present any issues of fact.

As set forth in the Brief on Behalf of Appellant, the lawfulness of the order was certainly not "clear as a matter of law."[11] (App. Br. at 24-28.)

> *Note 1.* When it is **clear as a matter of law** that the order was lawful, this should be resolved as an interlocutory question, and the

[10] Strangely, the government presents a combined argument in answer to Assignments of Error VII and VIII; then the government segregates its "combined" argument such that subsection A of the combined argument addresses Assignment of Error VIII (lawfulness of the order) while subsection B of the combined argument addresses Assignment of Error VII (military judge failing to permit members to hear evidence on unlawfulness of order).

[11] Contrast Assignment of Error VIII in the Brief on Behalf of Appellant with the absence of any discussion on the lawfulness of the substance of the order in the government's brief. If the order is clear as a matter of law, why does the government brief fail to so demonstrate?

members should be advised as follows:

Benchbook, para. 3-29 (emphasis added).

As set forth in the reply argument to Assignment of Error VIIIA, *infra*, the government does not even attempt to contest the unlawfulness of the order. Instead, the government merely asserts that the order's lawfulness or unlawfulness is beyond the reach of the court-martial and this Court because it involves a nonjusticiable political question. Thus, by the government's own theory of the case, it is certainly not "clear as a matter of law" that the order was lawful. At best, under the government's theory of the case, the lawfulness or unlawfulness of the order was nonjusticiable. In any event, the government's first assumption that the lawfulness of the order was "clear as a matter of law" is unwarranted.

The government's second assumption that the determination concerning the lawfulness of the order did not present any issues of fact is similarly unwarranted. The Brief on Behalf of Appellant sets forth at least 16 factual issues surrounding the lawfulness of the order. (App. Br. at 26-27 citing R. at 442-444.)

When facts are an issue with respect to the lawfulness of an order, the facts must be resolved by the members:

> *Note 2*. If there is a **factual dispute as to whether or not the order was lawful**, that dispute must be **resolved by the members** in connection with their determination of guilt or innocence. The following instruction should be given in cases where the military judge concludes that the lawfulness of the order presents an issue of fact for determination by the members.

Benchbook, para. 3-29 (emphasis added).

The military judge's determination solely by himself that

the order was lawful violated SPC New's right to be tried by members and other important constitutional rights. (App. Br. at 27-28.) The military judge's failure in this regard is of a constitutional magnitude. See *United States v. Brooks*, *supra*, at 180; *United States v. Webster*, *supra*; *and United States v. Hicks*, *supra*.

VIII

THE MILITARY JUDGE ERRED BY FINDING THAT THE ORDER WAS LAWFUL.[12]

A. The Government Does Not Seriously Contest the Unlawfulness of the Order to Deploy in the UN Uniform.

Instead of defending, or even discussing, the lawfulness of the order to deploy to Macedonia in the UN Uniform, the government brief adopts the remarkable position that the government may court-martial SPC New for disobeying a lawful order dealing with foreign policy, but SPC New may not defend against the lawfulness of the order, because to do so would involve a nonjusticiable political question. In other words, the government's position is this: If, in an Article 92 prosecution, litigation of the lawfulness of the order would involve foreign policy matters, the government need only prove a violation of an order, not a violation of a *lawful* order.

In this manner, the government seeks to rewrite Article 92 by deleting the lawfulness requirement for the order and prohibiting SPC New from defending on the grounds that the order was not lawful; to contest the lawfulness of the order is off limits because it treads on the forbidden ground of a nonjusticiable political question. Thus, in the government's reasoning, when an order touches on foreign policy, an order's

---

[12] The Appellant reasserts and invites the Court's examination of *Grostefon* Issue I. (App. Br. at A-1-1 through A-1-8.)

presumption of lawfulness becomes an irrebuttable presumption; the doctrine of the nonjusticiability of political questions supercedes SPC New's constitutional rights to defend himself and require the government to prove each element of an offense beyond a reasonable doubt. Under the government's reasoning, the Constitution yields to a superior notion: the nonjusticiability of political questions.

Why does the government rely on the nonjusticiability of political questions instead of simply demonstrating that the order was lawful? The answer is obvious: With the exception of the judge advocate who briefed SPC New and his battalion and then later prosecuted SPC New, no government attorney anywhere will defend the government's proposition at trial that the UNPROFOR Macedonian mission was undertaken pursuant to UN Charter Chapter VI, thereby rendering it legal under UNPA Section 7[13].

UNPA Section 6 prohibits United States participation in UN Charter Chapter VII actions except pursuant to a specific agreement which has been approved by Congress. Congress has never approved any such agreement concerning the Macedonian deployment. The UN has placed formal reliance on UN Charter Chapter VII for its operation in Macedonia; the UN Security Council invoked Chapter VII in passing several resolutions concerning the UNPROFOR Macedonian mission. At no time did the UN Security Council ever refer to UN Charter Chapter VI with respect to the UNPROFOR Macedonian mission. Given the UN's consistent references to the Macedonian operation as a UN Charter Chapter VII operation and the total absence of UN references to the Macedonian operation as a UN Charter Chapter VI operation, any contention that the Macedonian operation was undertaken pursuant to UN Charter Chapter VI, and correspondingly UNPA Section 7, is disingenuous. (App. Br. at 32-41.)

As set forth in the Brief on Behalf of Appellant (App. Br. at

[13] UNPA Section 6 governs the use of military power that proceeds from UN Charter Chapter VII, while UNPA section 7 relates to UN Charter Chapter VI concerning noncombatant assistance, i.e. UNPA Section 6 relates to Chapter VII, while UNPA Section 7 relates to Chapter VI.

39-41), President Clinton lied to Congress in two letters to the Speaker of the House dated July 9, 1993 and January 8, 1994 by stating that the UNPROFOR mission in Macedonia was authorized by UN Charter Chapter VI and UNPA Section 7.[14] The President lied in order to avoid the strict constraints of UNPA Section 6 which required him to obtain approval from Congress *prior* to deployment of any American soldiers in a UN Charter Chapter VII armed force operation. Because he wished to avoid obtaining prior approval from Congress, the President deceitfully mischaracterized the Macedonian operation as one authorized by UN Charter Chapter VI and UNPA Section 7 instead of truthfully denominating it as an operation under UN Charter Chapter VII and UNPA Section 6. (App. Br. at 39-41.)

The President's deceitful letters, drafted for political purposes to avoid the rigors of congressional scrutiny prior to the deployment of American soldiers in a UN operation, serve as the genesis of the chain of events which led to SPC New's court-martial. In turn, President Clinton's deception led the briefing judge advocate to inaccurately assert to SPC New and his battalion that their deployment to Macedonia was authorized by the UNPA and, hence, lawful. Other than the briefing judge advocate's inaccurate assertion to SPC New and his battalion, as well as the same judge advocate's later similar assertions at SPC New's court-martial, no government attorney has attempted to defend the lawfulness of the order by appealing to UN Charter Chapter VI and UNPA Section 7. Certainly, the government has declined to do so anywhere in its brief[15]. (App. Br. at 32-41.)

Consequently, the government's brief does not persist in advocating the legality of the deployment of American sol-

[14] See Brief on Behalf of Appellant, Appendix IV, for President Clinton's letters to the Speaker of the House.

[15] Of course, this Court can utilize its fact-finding power and hold that the UNPROFOR operation in Macedonia was undertaken pursuant to UN Charter Chapter VI and UNPA Section 7 or, alternatively, hold as a matter of law that the operation was a UN Charter Chapter VI and UNPA Section 7 operation. The appellant doubts that the government can persuade this Court to do so inasmuch as there is no basis for such a factual or legal conclusion. Certainly, the government has not attempted to advance any such basis in its brief.

diers to Macedonia as having been established under UN Charter Chapter VI and authorized by UNPA Section 7. Instead, the government attempts to dodge the entire matter by devising three points in its answer to Assignment of Error VIII:

a. The lawfulness of the order to SPC New is off the judicial table and beyond discussion because the matter is a nonjusticiable political question. (Resp. Br. at 16-24.);

b. The lawfulness of the deployment is immaterial because only the lawfulness of the order to wear the UN Uniform was an issue at SPC New's court-martial. (Resp. Br. at 21-23); and

c. The order to SPC New must have been lawful because Congress failed to impeach President Clinton or take other corrective action concerning the Macedonian deployment. (Resp. Br. at 2 1-23.)

With respect to the government's first device to avoid litigating the legality of the deployment (nonjusticiability), see Section VIIIB, *infra*.

With respect to the government's second device to avoid litigating the legality of the deployment (immateriality of the deployment), see the discussion in the Brief on Behalf of Appellant concerning the requirement for a nexus between a military duty to obey an order and a legitimate military purpose. An order is not lawful if it does not relate to a valid military purpose. (App. Br. at 30-31.)

> Without the legitimacy and legality of the deployment to Macedonia in UN Uniform, LTC Layfield possessed no more authority to order SPC New to don the UN Uniform than he would have had to, say, order SPC New to walk around in baby blue leotards, or to cross-dress as a transvestite, or to wear a swastika on his headgear, or to dress in a

white hood and a white sheet. The deployment and the order to don the UN Uniform
were inextricably linked; if the deployment is
illegal, LTC Layfield's order to don the UN
Uniform had no military purpose, was illegit-
imate, was unlawful, and SPC New had no
duty to obey it.

(App. Br. at 31.)

With respect to the government's third device to avoid litigating the legality of the deployment (Congress did not
impeach the President), the government suggests a new test
for lawfulness: If Congress does not impeach the President,
the President must be acting lawfully. According to this test,
no court need directly examine the President's conduct concerning his official (or perhaps personal) conduct. All a court
would have to do is to query whether Congress had
impeached the President; if not, then the President's actions
would be lawful. Of course, the government's brief cites no
authority for this novel test for determining Executive Branch
compliance with statutes or the Constitution.

B. The Political Question Doctrine Did Not
Constrain the Court-Martial and Does Not
Constrain This Court from Deciding Any Issue
in this Case.

The government's contention that the issue of the legality of
the deployment of troops is a nonjusticiable political question
is without merit for three reasons: (1) the political question
doctrine has no application in Article I courts; the doctrine
operates as a limitation only on Article III courts; (2) questions of statutory interpretation are not political questions; (3)
this case presents no nonjusticiable political questions even
under the traditional norms for Article III courts deciding constitutional issues.

1. THE POLITICAL QUESTION DOCTRINE BINDS

ONLY ARTICLE III COURTS.

Courts-martial are not Article III federal courts. "Pursuant to Article I of the Constitution, Congress has established three tiers of military courts." *Weiss v. United States*, 510 U.S. 163, 166-167 (1994). See also, *Carter v. McClaughry*, 183 U.S. 365 (1901). Simply stated, military courts are part of the executive branch of government, not the judicial branch.

The political question doctrine has always been inextricably tied to Article III. The Supreme Court has labeled political questions among the "doctrines that cluster about Article III." *Allen v. Wright*, 468 U.S. 737, 750 (1984). See also. *United States v. Sisson*, 399 U.S. 267, 276 (1970) (linking the political question doctrine to an Article III limitation in the context of a case challenging the constitutionality of the Vietnam War); *Mahoney v. Babbitt*, 113 F.3d 219, 220 (D.C. Cir. 1997) (citing Article III as the source of the political question doctrine); *National Treasury Employees Union V. United States*, 101 F.3d 1423, 1427 (1996) (D.C. Cir. 1996) ("In an attempt to give meaning to Article III's case-or-controversy requirement, the courts have developed a series of principles termed 'justiciability doctrines,' among which are standing, ripeness, mootness, and the political question doctrine."); *Graham v. Butterworth*, 5 F.3d 496, 498-499 (11th Cir. 1993) (linking Article III to the political question doctrine as a limitation on the federal courts' power to "encroach upon the powers of other branches of government."); *No Gwen Alliance of Lane City v. Aldridge*, 855 F.2d 1380, 1382 (9th Cir. 1988) (the political question doctrine is a limitation on "federal courts, under Article III....").

Moreover, the reason for this limitation on Article III courts has been grounded in the principle of separation of powers. See, *Nixon v. United States*, 506 U.S. 224, 252 (1993) ("the political question doctrine is essentially a function of the separation of powers, existing to restrain courts from inappropriate interference in the business of the other branches of Government." (internal citations omitted)).

SPC New challenges the lawfulness of an order of the President concerning deployment. SPC New's court-martial and this Court are within the same branch of government as the President, not a different branch. There exists no separation of powers issue concerning the ability of the court-martial or this Court to declare an action of the President to have been unlawful. It may require courage for a military court to declare the Commander-in-Chief's order to be illegal, but no separation of powers issue arises from an Article I court holding that the executive branch has violated the statutes of the United States.

It is true, as the government points out in its brief, that the United States Court of Appeals for the Armed Forces relied on the political question doctrine as an alternate holding in *United States v. Huet-Vaughn*, 43 M.J. 105, 114 (1995). However, this reliance was essentially *dicta*. In the briefs filed by Huet-Vaughn's counsel, no issue was raised about the legality of the decision to employ military forces in the Persian Gulf. Therefore, the Court's observation in *Huet-Vaughn* that the employment of military forces in the Persian Gulf was a political question was simply immaterial to the issues which had actually been raised in the case. In *Huet-Vaughn*, the Court assumed, but did not decide, that the political question doctrine had pertinency in Article I courts. The matter was briefed only in the most perfunctory manner by the government,[16] and not at all for Huet-Vaughn. To the extent that *Huet-Vaughn* held that Article I courts are bound by the political question constraints of Article III federal courts, that decision is not binding precedent since it conflicts with the clear holdings of the United States Supreme Court to the contrary.

The political question doctrine remains applicable to only

---

[16] See, government brief in *Huet-Vaughn* at 11-12.

Article III courts.

2. QUESTIONS OF STATUTORY INTERPRETATION ARE NOT POLITICAL QUESTIONS.

SPC New argues that the order to wear the UN Uniform violates a law of Congress which prohibits the acceptance of an office (UN soldier) and decorations (insignia, etc.) from a foreign government. 5 U.S.C. § 7342. He also argues that this order violates the military's own regulations. AR 670-1. He further argues that the order to deploy him as a UN soldier in a UN Uniform under foreign command violates the UNPA.

The Supreme Court has forthrightly declared that questions of statutory interpretation—even those which touch on foreign affairs—are not barred by the political question doctrine.

> We address first the Japanese petitioners' contention that the present actions are unsuitable for judicial review because they involve foreign relations and that a federal court, therefore, lacks the judicial power to command the Secretary of Commerce, an Executive Branch official, to dishonor and repudiate an international agreement. Relying on the political question doctrine, and quoting *Baker v. Carr*, 369 U.S. 186, 217 (1962), the Japanese petitioners argue that the danger of "embarrassment from multifarious pronouncements by various departments on one question" bars any judicial resolution of the instant controversy.

> We disagree. *Baker* carefully pointed out that not every matter touching on politics is a political question, id., at 209, and more specifically, that it is "error to suppose that every case or controversy which touches foreign relations lies beyond judicial cog-

nizance." Id., at 211. The political question doctrine excludes from judicial review those controversies which revolve around policy choices and value determinations constitutionally committed for resolution to the halls of Congress or the confines of the Executive Branch. The Judiciary is particularly ill suited to make such decisions, as "courts are fundamentally underequipped to formulate national policies or develop standards for matters not legal in nature." *United States ex rel. Joseph v. Cannon*, 206 U. S. App. D. C. 405, 411, 642 F.2d 1373, 1379 (1981) (footnote omitted), cert. denied, 455 U.S. 999 (1982).

As *Baker* plainly held, however, the courts have the authority to construe treaties and executive agreements, and it goes without saying that interpreting congressional legislation is a recurring and accepted task for the federal courts. It is also evident that the challenge to the Secretary's decision not to certify Japan for harvesting whales in excess of IWC quotas presents a purely legal question of statutory interpretation. The Court must first determine the nature and scope of the duty imposed upon the Secretary by the Amendments, a decision which calls for applying no more than the traditional rules of statutory construction, and then applying this analysis to the particular set of facts presented below. We are cognizant of the interplay between these Amendments and the conduct of this Nation's foreign relations, and we rec-

ognize the premier role which both Congress
and the Executive play in this field. But
under the Constitution, one of the Judiciary's
characteristic roles is to interpret statutes,
and we cannot shirk this responsibility merely because our decision may have significant
political overtones. We conclude, therefore,
that the present cases present a justiciable
controversy, and turn to the merits of peti-
tioners' arguments.

Japanese Whaling Ass'n v. American Cetacean Society, 478 U.S. 221, 229-230 (1986).

See also, *Population Institute v. McPherson*, 797 F.2d 1062, 1079 (D.C. Cir. 1986) ("Although the district court appeared to view this as an nonjusticiable political question [citation omitted], it is rather in our view purely an issue of statutory interpretation."); *Sioux Valley Empire Elec. Assn v. Butz*, 504 F.2d 168, 172 (8th Cir. 1974) ("The question involved is one of statutory interpretation and the issue [citation omitted] is justiciable.").

Questions of statutory interpretation and compliance have been held to be justiciable in the federal courts even against the military. See, *Harmon v. Brucker*, 355 U.S. 579 (1958) (per curiam). "*Harmon* explicitly resolved the issue of whether the courts have power to review nonconstitutional claims." Note, JUDICIAL REVIEW OF CONSTITUTION-AL CLAIMS AGAINST THE MILITARY, 84 Colum.

L.Rev. 387, 390, fn. 17 (1984). See, *Beard v. Stahr*, 370 U.S. 41, 44 (1962): "When the Army departs from the statu-tory standard which prescribes the basis on which discharges will be issued, the federal courts can intervene." See, also *Leedom v. Kyne*, 358 U.S. 184, 190 (1958).

In *Dilley v. Alexander*, 603 F.2d 914 (D.C. Cir. 1979), the Court specifically rejected a request for special deference to the military in a case brought by officers claiming they had been discharged illegally:

> It is a basic tenet of our legal system that a government agency is not at liberty to ignore its own laws and that agency action in contravention of applicable statutes and regulations is unlawful. The military departments enjoy no immunity from this proscription. It is the duty of the federal courts to inquire whether an action of a military agency conforms to the law, or is instead arbitrary, capricious, or contrary to the statutes and regulations governing that agency. The logic of these cases derives from the self-evident proposition that the Government must obey its own laws.

603 F.2d at 920. (Internal citations omitted). See also, *Metzenbaum v. Federal Energy Regulatory Com'n*, 675 F.2d 1282, 1287 (D.C. Cir. 1982).

SPC New's claim that the order of deployment violates the UNPA requires nothing more than statutory interpretation, and perhaps interpretation of the treaty called the United Nations Charter, but these are precisely the kinds of issues that were held justiciable in *Japanese Whaling Ass'n*.

SPC New's case does not present the kind of constitutional question that arises when a soldier argues that a particular deployment was an act of war requiring a congressional declaration of war. With the UNPA, Congress has created a statute controlling the President's actions in assigning American soldier to fight for the United Nations. It is the duty of the courts to determine if the President has complied with this statute when a soldier is tried by court-martial for disobeying a *lawful* order.

3. THE ISSUES IN THIS CASE ARE JUSTICIABLE

EVEN UNDER STANDARDS FOR CONSTITUTIONAL
CASES ARISING IN ARTICLE III COURTS.

While the government purports to rely on *Baker v. Carr*,
369 U.S. 186 (1962) to support its nonjusticiability argument,
such reliance is misplaced. In *Baker*, the Supreme Court
warned against categorical or *per se* arguments based on
broad proclamations by the judiciary. Instead, the Court ruled
that political question analysis requires a careful case-by-case
approach.

> There are sweeping statements to the effect
> that all questions touching foreign relations
> are political questions . . . . Yet it is error to
> suppose that every case or controversy which
> touches foreign relations lies beyond judicial
> cognizance.

369 U.S. at 211.

> The cases we have reviewed show the neces-
> sity for discriminating inquiry into the pre-
> cise facts and posture of the particular case,
> and the impossibility of resolution by any
> semantic cataloging.

369 U.S. at 217.

Yet, contrary to these teachings, the government employs
almost nothing other than "sweeping statements" and "semantic cataloguing," replete with references to inapposite non-
military cases which address war powers resolutions and similar matters having nothing to do with criminal prosecutions,
much less the lawfulness of an order under Article 92, UCMJ.
Foreign policy matters, the government repeatedly argues, is
an area into which a court-martial and this Court may not
intrude, as if this disposes of the appeal.

a. *Military Questions Can Be Justiciable.*

There are six military cases concerning justiciability from

the Supreme Court. In four, the Supreme Court did not dismiss on political question grounds, but reached the merits: *Rostker v. Goldberg*, 453 U.S. 57 (1981) *Brown v. Glines*, 444 U.S. 348 (1980); *Burns v. Wilson*, 346 U.S. 137 (1953); *Orloff v. Willoughby*, 345 U.S. 83 (1953). Clearly military cases are not categorically off limits.

b. *Foreign Policy Questions Can Be Justiciable.*

Any suggestion that foreign policy cases can be semantically catalogued as nonjusticiable was authoritatively rejected by the Supreme Court in *Baker v. Carr*, *supra* at 211. In *Crockett v. Reagan*, 558 F. Supp. 893 (D.D.C. 1982); *aff'd*, 720 F.2d 1355 (D.C. Cir.), *cert. denied*, 467 U.S. 1251 (1984), the Court expressly rejected the blanket "hands-off of foreign policy" dogma urged by the Government.

> The Court **disagrees** with defendants that this is the type of political question which involves potential judicial interference with executive discretion in the foreign affairs field. Plaintiffs do not seek relief that would dictate foreign policy but rather to enforce existing law concerning the procedures for decision-making. Moreover, the issue here is not a political question simply because it involves the apportionment of power between the executive and legislative branches. **The duty of courts to decide such questions has been repeatedly affirmed by the Supreme Court**.

Id. at 898 (emphasis added).

c. *SPC New's Claims Differ from Vietnam Cases.*

The government relies heavily on Vietnam War cases for its contention that all cases touching military deployment are nonjusticiable.

A cursory review of the Vietnam War cases, however, demonstrates that the issues raised in SPC New's case are different. In the Vietnam cases, claims were not based upon a contention, as here, that the President had violated a specific military regulation or Congressional statute. Rather, those claims were based upon one fundamental allegation that the Constitution required Congress to formally declare war before the President had any authority to utilize military force in Vietnam. See *Mora v. McNamara*, 389 U.S. 934, 934-35 (1967) (Stewart. J. dissenting). The issues raised by such a contention might very well be nonjusticiable. See *Id.*, 389 U.S. at 935-38 (Douglas, J. dissenting), although the Court has in the past addressed the question on the merits. *Prize Cases*, 67 U.S. (2 Black) 635 (1863).

In contrast to the broad, sweeping constitutional questions concerning the general allocation of war power between Congress and the President, the constitutional questions raised by SPC New are well-defined and narrow, and concern separation of powers questions that are controlled by explicit textual provisions.

d. *A Detailed Inquiry into the Baker Standards Demonstrates that the Issues in SPC New's Case are Justiciable.*

Even though most of the questions raised by SPC New concern the interpretation of statutory or regulatory provisions which are clearly justiciable, the "discriminating inquiry" required in constitutional matters by the threefold *Baker v. Carr* standard, as summarized by Justice Powell in *Goldwater v. Carter*, 444 U.S. 996, 998 (1979), demonstrates that all of the legal and constitutional issues raised in SPC New's case are justiciable.

(1) "Does the issue involve resolution of questions committed by the text of the Constitution to a coordinate branch of Government?" *Goldwater v. Carter, supra*, at 998.

At the heart of SPC New's case, there exists a conflict between laws enacted by Congress and an order issued by the President. Resolution of a legal dispute between the President and the Congress is a duty that has been textually committed to the judiciary. *Marbury v. Madison*, 5 U.S. 1 (1803).

The first issue raised by SPC New is whether the President's order to deploy as a UN Soldier in a UN Uniform violates the UNPA. 22 U.S.C. § 287d. SPC New is clearly in the class of citizens to be protected by the UNPA which expressly prohibits the President from placing American soldiers into military service under the UN without the approval of Congress.

This statute is squarely based on Congress's Article I § 8 power to "make rules for the government and regulation of the land and naval forces." Congress's power to make such regulations is plenary and the courts are duty-bound to enforce the will of Congress even when the President takes opposing action on the subject. This is true regardless of whether the matter is characterized as a military issue or foreign policy. *Rostker v. Goldberg, supra*; *Youngstown Sheet & Tube Co. v. Sawyer*, 343 U.S. 579 (1952). The President cannot claim any exclusive commitment from the text of the Constitution here.

The second issue raised by SPC New is whether he can be ordered to serve under foreign commanders in light of the Appointments Clause (Article II § 2). SPC New does not challenge a discretionary management decision concerning the military's appointed officers as in *Arnheiter v. Chafee*, 435 F.2d 691 (9th Cir. 1970), a matter which is textually committed to the President. Rather, SPC New's case asks this Court to decide whether the President can unilaterally avoid the Appointments Clause and relevant statutes by commanding American soldiers to serve under a military officer commissioned by a foreign government not in accordance with the constitutional and statutory procedures for commissioning American military officers. See *Weiss v. United States*, 510

U.S. 163, 127 L.Ed.2d 1, 11(1994). Whatever the power of the President may be in a situation like World War II when he acts under a declaration of war by Congress, one of the principal reasons why Congress enacted the UNPA was to avoid the possibility that American soldiers would be placed under UN command without congressional consent. When Congress provides for the appointment of officers to exercise executive power and the claim is that an appointment has departed from the constitutional process, the case is appropriate for judicial review. *Buckley v. Valeo*, 424 U.S. 1, 118-143 (1976). The case for justiciability can be no different for a claim that the President has ignored the Appointments Clause. Again, the President cannot claim any exclusive commitment from the text of the Constitution here.

The third issue raised by SPC New involves the specific command to become a UN soldier who wears the UN Uniform. The relevant textual commitment, Article I § 9, is to Congress, not to the President. Congress has employed its power to specifically ban the acceptance of the office (UN soldier) and decorations (insignia) by federal employees. 5 U.S.C. § 7342. The question of whether the UN is a foreign power for these purposes has been resolved because Congress has expressly decided the question. 5 U.S.C. § 7342(a)(2). The relevant military regulations which ban acceptance and use of foreign insignia on the battle dress uniform are clearly justiciable under the previously-cited precedents requiring the military to obey its own rules. Again, no exclusive constitutional textual commitment lies in favor of the President here.

The final issue raised by SPC New[17], whether he can be denied a crucial attribute of his citizenship—overriding his right and duty to be singularly loyal to the United States—raises no issues committed by the Constitution's text to the President or the military. Indeed, the Supreme Court has expressly held that the military may not make final determi-

---

[17] See Brief on Behalf of Appellant, Appendix I - *Grostefon Issue I*. (App. Br. at A-1-1 through A-1-8.) SPC New again requests that this Court direct the government to brief this important *Grostefon* issue.

nations about a soldier's citizenship. *Trop v. Dulles*, 356 U.S. 86 (1958), see especially, Black, concurring, *Id.* 356 U.S. at 104. Regulation of citizenship is textually committed to Congress, not the President. See Article I § 8 and Fourteenth Amendment §§ 1 and 5.

In none of the salient issues raised by SPC New is there any exclusive constitutional textual commitment to the President.

(2) "Would resolution of the question demand that a court move beyond areas of judicial expertise?" *Goldwater v. Carter*, *supra*, at 998.

In a demonstration of duplicity which should not be condoned by any court, the government has adopted directly contrary advocacy positions in this Court and in the federal courts addressing SPC New's *habeas* case: In the federal courts, the government argues that the Article III courts should defer to the special expertise of the military courts; in this Court, the government argues that the Article III political question doctrine should be employed to prevent this Court from exercising that special expertise. Thus, all the courthouse doors are barred to SPC New.

In *Gilligan v. Morgan*, 413 U.S. 1 (1975) the Court held that it would transcend the expertise of the federal judiciary to assume responsibility for the day-to-day operation of the Ohio National Guard. This broad request led to dismissal on grounds of judicial unmanageability. The Court warned, however, that its decision should not be read to announce a *per se* rule.

> In concluding that no justiciable controversy is presented, it should be clear that we neither hold nor imply that the conduct of the National Guard is always beyond judicial review or that there may not be accountability in a judicial forum for violations of law or for specific unlawful conduct by military

personnel. . . .

Id. 11-12.

By deciding the issues in SPC New's case, this Court does not assume daily operation of any military unit. All that must be done is to read and interpret a federal statute, examine the UN documents to determine which article was used to authorize this military force, and determine whether or not Congress has passed a formal approval of this use of American soldiers. Every one of these decisions can be made from reading documents and statutes. No trips to Macedonia are required. No unmanageable standards are suggested by the government. This *Baker* standard, even if applicable, clearly falls in favor of justiciability.

(3) "Do prudential considerations counsel against judicial intervention?" *Goldwater v. Carter, supra*, at 998.

The government broadly asserts, without explanation, that a decision on the lawfulness of the order to deploy would foster "multifarious pronouncements by various departments" of government (Resp. Br. at 17, 23 quoting *Baker v. Carr, supra*). The government contends: "That is, based upon the constitutional principal of **separation of powers in the three branches of government**, judicial review of 'political questions' is precluded..." (Resp. Br. at 17, emphasis added.) Again, this Court is not another branch of government; this is an Article I court.

Moreover, the respect due the President, under the circumstances of this case, must take into account that he has acted in direct violation of the Acts of Congress and has lied to Congress concerning his actions. As Justice Jackson stated in his concurring opinion in *Youngstown Sheet & Tube*, 343 U.S. at 637:

> When the President takes measures incompatible with the expressed . . . will of

> Congress, his power is at its lowest ebb, for
> then he can rely only upon his own constitu-
> tional powers minus any constitutional pow-
> ers of Congress over the matter.

See also *Dames & Moore v. Regan*, 453 U.S. 654, 669 (1981); *American International Group v. Islamic Republic of Iran*, 657 F.2d 430, 439 (D.C. Cir. 1981).

In *Powell v. McCormack*, 395 U.S. 486, 539 (1969) the Court rejected the suggestion that it should refrain from decid-ing the merits of that case because of "a potentially embar-rassing confrontation between coordinate branches of the Federal Government." The Court said, "Our system of gov-ernment requires that federal courts on occasion interpret the Constitution in a manner at variance with the construction given the document by another branch. The alleged conflict that such an adjudication may cause cannot justify the courts' avoiding their constitutional responsibility." 395 U.S. at 549.

Although the political question doctrine does not constrain this Court, even if it did, the duty to require obedience to the law and Constitution is a higher value as has been clear from the earliest days of the Republic.

> This doctrine would subvert the very founda-
> tion of all written constitutions. It would
> declare that an act which, according to the
> principles and theory of our government, is
> entirely void, is yet, in practice completely
> obligatory.... It is prescribing limits, and
> declaring that those limits may be passed at
> pleasure.

Marbury v. Madison, supra, 5 U.S. at 178.

As demonstrated by the threefold *Baker V. Carr* standard as summarized by Justice Powell in *Goldwater v. Carter* (444 U.S. at 998), all of the legal and constitutional issues raised in

SPC New's case are clearly justiciable.

IX

AN APPROVED SENTENCE THAT INCLUDES A BAD CONDUCT DISCHARGE FOR SPC NEW'S OFFENSE IS INAPPROPRIATELY SEVERE.

The government contends that "[SPC New] received only a punitive discharge." (Resp. Br. at 30) (emphasis added). The use of the modifier "only" to suggest that a punitive discharge is not inappropriately severe under the facts of this case badly distorts and unfairly ignores the severity of a punitive discharge as a punishment.

The severity of a punitive discharge as a sentence is well-established. The Court of Appeals for the Armed Forces has long recognized the ineradicable stigma of a punitive discharge.

> The severity of these penalties, unknown to civil life as they are, cannot be denied. . . [T]he ordering of a punitive discharge so characterizes an individual that his whole future is utterly destroyed. He is marked far beyond the civilian felon, hampered as he may be by the sneering term "ex-con," for, justifiedly or not, the punitive discharge so dishonors and disgraces an accused that he finds employment virtually impossible; is subjected to many legal deprivations; and is regarded with horror by his fellow citizens. Truly, it has come to be the modern equivalent of the ancient practice of branding felons, and the stain it leaves is as ineradica-

> ble. And, in the case of a soldier with extend-
> ed service, the discharge can be even more
> severe, for, as the Chief Judge wisely noted
> [citation omitted] "an executed punitive dis-
> charge terminates military status as com-
> pletely as an executed death penalty ends
> mortal life."

United States v. Wheeler, 17 USCMA 274, 38 CMR 72 (1967).

When one considers the extent to which SPC New will suf-fer from his court-martial sentence for the rest of his life and the employment opportunities which he will be denied by virtue of his conviction alone, to argue that his sentence is appropriate because he received "only" a bad-conduct dis-charge strains credulity.

In addition, the government's characterization of SPC New's charged misconduct as "flagrant disobedience" contra-dicts the facts of this case. The word "flagrant" is defined as "extremely, flauntingly, or purposefully conspicuous, usu. because of **uncommon evil, unworthiness, unpleasantness, or truculence ...**" Webster's Third New International Dictionary (1981) (emphasis added).

As the record demonstrates, SPC New's actions were not "flagrant" in any sense. He did not refuse to deploy with his unit. He did not refuse to pick up a weapon and defend his country. He did not commit, and was not charged with, will-ful disrespect. He did not foment disorder or notoriously chal-lenge the legitimacy of his command to order him to deploy. He merely wore the uniform of the United States Army, not the UN Uniform. Although his motive may not constitute a defense to the charge, the circumstances surrounding his offense certainly bear scrutiny as mitigating circumstances.[18]

---

[18] The government urges this Court to disregard matters presented pursuant to R.C.M. 1105 in assessing the severity of SPC New's sentence. (Resp. Br. at 30-31.) However, as the appellant made his request pursuant to *United States v. Grostefon*, 12 M.J. 431 (C.M.A. 1982) (App. Br. at 48, note 21), those matters are properly before this Court for consideration and cannot be disre-garded.

WHEREFORE, the appellant respectfully requests that this Court set aside the findings and the sentence.

HENRY HAMILTON, P.A.
Civilian Defense Counsel
Ratchford & Associates
1531 Laurel Street
Columbia, South Carolina
  29201-2697
(803) 779-0700

PAUL FIORINO
Captain. JA
Appellate Defense Counsel
5611 Columbia Pike
Falls Church, Virginia 22041
(703) 681-3593

CERTIFICATE OF SERVICE AND FILING

I certify that a copy of the foregoing was personally delivered to this Honorable Court and Government Appellate Division on this 6th day of March 1998.

PAUL FIORINO

PAUL FIORINO
Captain, JA
Defense Appellate Division

FOR FURTHER READING

For further research and reference, the reader will find the following sources of value. Many of these books have been mailed or handed to us over the past three years. Some of them come from my personal library, or my father's. Others we have purchased to increase our own knowledge, from more than one perspective. Inclusion of a title does not necessarily imply agreement with any statement in any book or video. Indeed, some are supplied from those who support the concept of a one world government.

Allen, Gary, *Say "No!" to the New World Order, the Attack on U.S. Sovereignty…and how to Keep America Independent*, Concord Press, Seal Beach, California, 1987

Baker, Jeffrey – *Cheque Mate, the Game of Princes, The New World Order: Dark Conspiracy or Benevolent Master Plan – How it Affects You and the Sovereignty of America*. The Baker Group, St. Petersburg, Florida, 1993.

Brooke, Tal, *When the World Will Be As One, The Coming New World Order*, Harvest House, Eugene, Oregon, 1989.

Butler, Eric D., *Censored History*, Australian League of Rights, Melbourne, 1978.

Coey, John Alan – *A Martyr Speaks*, Journal of the Late John Alan Coey, The Coey Family, 1994 edition. 246 pages. (An inspiring account of an American who turned down a commission in the U.S. military in Vietnam, in order to make his stand for freedom as a medic in the Rhodesian Light Infantry. Killed in Action, 1975.)

Commission on Global Governance – *A People's Response to*

Our Global Neighborhood – Boston Research Center for the 21st Century, 1995. 294 pages.

Epperson, *The Unseen Hand, An Introduction to the Conspiratorial View of History*, Publius Press, Tucson, Arizona, 1985.

Fisas, Vicen, *Blue Geopolitics*, The United Nations Reform and the Future of the Blue Helmets. Foreword by UNESCO Director-General Federico Mayor Zaragoza, Pluto Press, London, 1995. 184 pages. (One need not rely on the enemies of the U.N. for documentation of their agenda – there is plenty put out by the U.N. itself.)

Foreign Affairs magazine, July/August 1996, "Back to the Womb?" by Arthur Schlesinger, Jr. Sept/Oct 1997, "Has Democracy a Future?" by Arthur Schlesinger, Jr. Sept/Oct 1997 "The Real New World Order," by Anne-Marie Slaughter.

Funderburk, David B., *Betrayal of America*, Bush's Appeasement of Communist Dictators Betrays American Principles. By a former ambassador to Rumania, and congressman, here is an author who has seen much of the inside of what happens in diplomatic circles. McDonald, 1991. Out of print.

Gurudas – *Treason – The New World Order*. Cassandra Press, San Rafael, California, 1996. 312 pages. (This is the first book, to our knowledge, to mention Michael New and his case.)

Jasper, William F. – *Global Tyranny…Step By Step, The United Nations and the Emerging New World Order*. Western Islands, Appleton, Wisconsin, 1992. 350 pages.

Kincaid, Cliff – *Global Taxes for World Government* – Huntington House Publishers, Lafayette, Louisiana, 1996. 200 pages.

Kinman, Dwight L. – *The World's Last Dictator*. Whitaker

House, Springdale, Pennsylvania, 1995. 319 pages.

McManus, John F. – *Changing Commands, The Betrayal of America's Military.* The John Birch Society, Appleton, Wisconsin, 1995. 233 pages.

McManus, John F. – *The Insiders*, Architects of the New World Order, The John Birch Society, Appleton, Wisconsin, 1995.

Nock, Albert Jay – *Our Enemy, the State* – 1944. Hallberg Publishing, Delavan, Wisconsin, 1994 edition.

Paolini & Jarvis, editors, *Between Sovereignty and Global Governance*, The United Nations, the State, and Civil Society, St. Martins Press, New York, 1998. This is a pro-United Nations publication.

Penabaz, Dr. Fernando – *What Do You Know About U.N.O.?*, Christian Crusade, 1967. (This old book shows that there were those who understood the threat to freedom and national sovereignty thirty years ago.)

Perloff, James – *The Shadows of Power* – Western Islands, Appleton. 1988, 1994. 264 pages.

Quigley, Carroll, *Tragedy & Hope, A History of the World in Our Time*, MacMillan, New York, 1966.

Roberts, Major Arch E. – *Victory Denied...Why Your Son Faces Death in "NO-WIN WARS."* – Committee to Restore the Constitution, Ft. Collins, 1966.

Stormer, John – *None Dare Call It Treason* Liberty Bell Press, Florissant, Missouri, 1964.

Stormer, John – *None Dare Call It Treason – 25 Years Later* – Liberty Bell Press, Florissant, Missouri, 1990, 1992. 625 pages.

Tarpley, Webster Griffin and Chaitkin, Antonin – *George Bush – The Unauthorized Biography*, Executive Intelligence Review, Washington, D.C., 1992. 659 pages. (Very unauthorized.)

Thorin, Duane – *The Pugwash Movement and U.S. Arms Policy*, "Should Weapons Systems be placed under International Control?", Monte Cristo Press, New York, 1965. 99 pages.

United Nations, 1996: *Disarmament at a Critical Juncture*, Panel discussions organized by the NGO Committee on Disarmament, United Nations, New York, 1997.

United Nations, *The World Conferences*, Developing Priorities for the 21st Century, United Nations, New York, 1997.

United Nations, UNITED NATIONS PUBLICATIONS, Catalogue 1997-1998, United Nations, New York, 1997.

U.S. Department of State, *Freedom From War, The United States Program for General and Complete Disarmament in a Peaceful World.* Department of State Publication 7277, 1961.

Veon, Joan – *Prince Charles, The Sustainable Prince*, Hearthstone, Oklahoma City, 1998. (Journalist Joan Veon has gone to almost every United Nations conference around the world for many years, and researches her work thoroughly, with excellent documentation.)

Veon, Joan – *The United Nations – and its Global Agenda for the Environment, Economy and Family*, Women's International Media Group, Olney, Md.

Wardner, Dr. James W. – *Unholy Alliances, The Secret Plan and the Secret People Who Are Working to Destroy America*, self published, 1997. 304 pages.

Watts, V. Orval – *The United Nations, Planned Tyranny* Comments on the Dream and the Reality, Devin-Adair, New York, 1955. (Forty years ago there were voices articulating the threat.)

Zahner, Dee – *The Secret Side of History*, LTAA Communications, Hesperia, California, 1994